Lessons from the F*%#ing Master

From the authors of "The Sex Seminar: Are you ready for the Red Pill?

IAM Center, LLC

Copyright 2014

To all the Teachers and Masters who without their guidance and inspiration this book could not have happened:

Dr. Ahwanetta Venteres, Rev. Knudsen, Stamatios Hiotakis, Katherine Traub, Joanne Robinson, Eddie Maldonado, Professor Lawrence Rosenfield, PhD, Professor Judith Summerfield, and Michael Rosker

Table of Contents

1. You're Worthless…Now Read this Book!
2. Shut the Fuck up and Listen
3. Are you Likeable?
4. What is Sexy?
5. The Beauty
6. The Unholy Triangle

As long as your worth is based on something external then you might as well be worthless.
    Fucking Master

You're Worthless...Now Read this Book!

Trinity: The other day you said we need to write a book called, "You're Worthless, now Read the Book."

Fucking Master: No not *the* book. "You're Worthless Now read THIS book."

Trinity: (Laughter) . . . and I find that's so harsh! I don't agree with the assumption of the premise. How could you possibly say someone's worthless? They're not worthless . . . **people are not worthless**, but you're telling them they're worthless.

Fucking Master: I'm telling them the truth. There are many individuals out in the world who are hiding the fact that they feel worthless. They lie to you, me, and themselves while arguing their worth. In the meantime they're scrambling around, chasing worth . . . they're worthless; they have no worth! They don't feel their worth. So, if I were them . . . I'd accept it; embrace it, "I'm worthless," now let's help you find your *real* value, your *real* worth.

Trinity: **But that doesn't mean they're worthless . . .**

Fucking Master: Yes it does! As long as you don't see yourself you're worthless.

Trinity: I . . . I just . . . I have such a problem with that word; is it a play on words thing?

Fucking Master: No; I mean it literally.

If you think you're stupid, you're going to behave and act stupidly. Your brain is not going to function as well; you're going to mumble, for instance, when you're trying to communicate . . . when you have something to say. You may not even speak it because you won't think it's worthwhile . . . if you think you're stupid, then, you're stupid! If you think you're worthless, then you're worthless.

Trinity: See, now you really got me going here because . . . NO, I think there's a lot of people that believe they're stupid because of the disempowering messages they were given as children by their families. Or, excuse my French, from "fucked up" teachers or crappy school systems . . . but *they're* not stupid!

Fucking Master: That was pretty stupid because that wasn't French!

Trinity: (Laughter) Anyways . . . they are not stupid; they might have a belief that they're stupid but I know that they're not stupid. These people are not worthless! I have friends that might not know their worth, but I don't believe they're worthless.

Fucking Master: That doesn't matter! If they think they're worthless, they're worthless. If they believe they're worthless, they're worthless. If you believe something, you're going to react from your belief, even if you're not what you believe.

Trinity: I could believe I'm a cat! It doesn't mean I am a cat . . .

Fucking Master: Right! But you're going to act like a freaking cat, licking yourself and drinking milk out of a dish. (Smiling) You're going to act like a cat. You're going to get a hundred cats and live with them. There are a lot of women out there that think they're cats and live with them, they're the big momma cats.

Trinity: That reminds me of people who think they're star people so they walk around being all like (weird voice) "Oh, I'm a star person, I'm not from here!" (Laughter)

Fucking Master: So now you're agreeing with me?

Trinity: No; it just kind of reminds me of that.

Fucking Master: No; I think you're starting to agree with me.

Trinity: (Laughter) Okay, I understand where you're coming from. I just found it harsh. I found the approach that you were taking to be harsh.

Fucking Master: If you're going to act like a dumbass, what do you expect me to say? "Oh excuse me, young person, it's not really nice to act like a dumbass . . ." No . . . "You're a fucking dumbass and you need to stop acting like a dumbass!" Okay? My message to them is . . . you're a dumbass, now let's inform you with the truth . . . come read this book and find out how **not** to be a dumbass."

Trinity: Okay . . . so how would **you** go about it then?

Fucking Master: You do it differently because you're the "mother type." I'm the "father type." I'm not going to do it so nicely, especially if the person's *that* entrenched in this illusion. When a person is really at bottom zero around their self worth, I'm not going to go soft at them. I'm going to say, "Yeah, you *are* absolutely worthless, but come on, let's do something about it!"

Trinity: Oh okay, I get your plan; I get what you're saying.

Fucking Master: So, what am I saying?

Trinity: Well, you're not quite the badass that you . . .

Fucking Master: No! Don't try to paint me into some nice Canadian!

Trinity: (Laughter) You actually do have a heart in there, somewhere.

Fucking Master: Please. You have to be with that I have a heart. (Teasing) I'm heartless.

Trinity: You're actually right on . . . I get your commitment to them.

Fucking Master: As long as your worth is based on something external then you might as well **be worthless.** Because this world is ever-changing, we're forever changing; the external world's forever changing . . . relying on these changeable elements for a stable sense of worth is insane. You're destined to feel like the stock market; up one day, down the next. So if your worth is in the mate you have, or your children, or your career, or your worth is in your intelligence, or based on your sexuality or your sexual prowess, on how hot you are . . . well that's going to eventually change! There's always someone who is and has more in any of these areas. You're going to be phased out, eventually, and someone else is going to come along and replace you and when that happens, your worth will diminish. It will always diminish if it's based on ANYTHING outside of you.

Trinity: I understand.

Fucking Master: If you do not get in touch with what is *authentic worth*--worth that transcends the physical world and cannot be diminished by time--if you're not in touch with **that** worth, then to me, you're worthless.

Now can I utilize you for things? Sure, I can utilize you as a transitory part of life and you can pack my bags at the supermarket . . .

Trinity: Oooh, that's not nice!

Fucking Master: Why not!? I mean I'm going to utilize you to pack my bags, if that's what you want.

Am I immune to the human that's in the body of the bag packer? NO, I can see the human that's in there I might even choose to reach in and help them become present to me . . . and in those shared moments they come to life. But, what you may not understand is as soon as I leave, if they're not self generated, they're going to go back to sleep and be a bag packer . . . so that's what they are!

Trinity: But what if . . . what about . . . Ugh, you just totally get my blood boiling!

There may be people that work in, say, Safeway, who are packing your bags and may be genuine. They may be wonderful people, they may be really gifted, intelligent--a genius even, you don't know. You don't know if they're artists when they go home, you don't know what kind of parent they are! You don't know anything about them, or their worth! If I may say, they may be worth more than a frigging lawyer, doctor, or president! How about that? Why is it that they don't have worth because they're packing your bags?

Fucking Master: (Smiling) You're too easy!

It has nothing to do with packing my bags; the lawyer can keep doing what he's doing for me, too. And if he doesn't understand his inner worth then he's worthless also. But, he's useful, you understand? He has utility, but not worth. For most of us, we've set ourselves up to have utility so we can be utilized. We can be utilized for sex; we can be utilized for our money, for our bag-packing ability, and for our legal skills. But utility doesn't give worth. It only leaves us with a temporary feeling of usefulness and when this feeling fades we're left empty. Of course, this leads us back to wanting to be utilized all over again! **It's an addiction!**

We can even be utilized as parents and mates while never feeling worthy of being either. For most people, they just utilize one another; it's utility. It has no basis in worth! What you describe as "worth," I call "utility." Your definition of worth is actually that of utility. Worth comes from something a lot different than superficial utility.

So, my doctor and lawyer can be utilized, but if he or she doesn't feel a sense of worth then they're worthless, but they can still be utilized; they have utility.

Trinity: I understand what you're saying. Where I have an issue with you is that you picked a person who works in a supermarket, packing grocery bags, as if they had less value than a doctor. But I have seen in grocery packers, more light and more life in their faces that I've seen in nurses or doctors in a hospital.

Fucking Master: Okay, I did not say all bag packers are worthless. I said if you're worthless, you can pack my bags.

I only picked the bag packer because I knew it would get under your skin. You like to fight on behalf of what you believe are the lowly. To me we're all lowly, if we're worthless. If we have not accessed our true worth, then we're worthless. It doesn't matter if we're talking about the President of the United States, the Prime Minister of Canada, or a bag packer at Safeway; if you base your worth on external means you're worthless. BUT, I'll utilize you if that's how you want to be used.

It's like the difference between self confidence and self esteem. Self confidence is a con job; self CONfidence. It's a confidence game we play on ourselves and on each other. Self confidence is something we have to work on daily. Every day, you have to con yourself into believing you're beautiful, smart, happy, able, powerful, etc. If you miss a day, your self confidence weakens. If someone speaks of you to the contrary, it lessens. You see, self confidence is strictly driven by the external. Whereas, self esteem is from within; it cannot be diminished through external means.

Unfortunately, I cannot use you with *value* if you don't experience it. I might have a sense of your value and appreciate it, but it's not going to be communicated to you. You won't get or want to get it. You'll have a kind of a block or a wall that stops you from experiencing your worth. There are people who, if you said to them, "You're worth more than that!" or you gave them more, let's say love or money . . . they'd eventually turn around and kick you in the ass. This is because you have made them aware of their previously hidden feelings of unworthiness. We often make someone feel worthless when we try to show them their worth because prior to that they were asleep to the fact that they felt worthless and you awoke them to it!

Trinity: Yes, they have to, then, feel their pain.

Fucking Master: Exactly! So, I don't bother them, I just utilize them the way they'd like to be utilized. "Okay! I'll utilize you if you don't want to play in the worth game with me!" I respect that, who am I to intrude? But I will say there's a book, and it will be called "You're Worthless, Now read this Book!" And, if you're in touch with any feelings of worthlessness then you can read it. At which point you'll be partway home because your interest is all it takes to begin. But, for the person who is either lying to themselves, or is, in fact, asleep to the fact that they're just being utilized and think they have worth, they're not going to read it; and that's no biggy. It's perfect actually, because

I can't do anything for them in the first place and neither can you.

Trinity: Okay, I now get where you're coming from . . .

Fucking Master: Yeah there is a huge difference between worth and utility; we can set ourselves up to be worth-full or utilized. This is easily observed on Facebook.

If you look at the pictures of young females and young males on Facebook, you'll notice just about every other picture, especially for females, is sexually oriented. It's about them in some sort of sexual pose, and commenting to one another about how hot they are, and how "hot your legs are . . . your lips are . . . or your ass is." Unfortunately, most of these young females think that their only sense of worth is their bodies and their sexuality. So, are they worthy? Or, are they someone to be utilized? For me, they're nothing but someone to be utilized and objectified; they're setting themselves up for that. They've communicated that their worth comes from their sexuality. Now, if there were a mixture of pictures, I'd be forced to think otherwise. But that's not the case; not for the majority of them.

Most of their pictures are sets of mimicked poses. They normally contain the classic "duck face" pose, which is a kissing pose, or body shaping poses that includes breast and ass presentations. And if you're wondering how I know this, it's not because I'm a creep. I don't go around looking at Facebook and all the girls; this is strictly for research purposes . . .

(Laughter)

The point is, if your worth is based on your body, alone, you're not going to understand or find your real true worth. Fortunately, you'll be utilized, but only until you're used up!

So, these are the future, cougars and MILF's, but not of the good kind. They're only in their teens and 20's now, but one day they'll be in their 30's, 40's, and 50's and they will still be relying on their sexuality. At that point it will be scary-spooky; now you'll have Lola, the Showgirl, on your hands. This will be sad because by this point they are likely to never find any self worth.

Trinity: I presume you're speaking of the *old* Barry Manilow song, *Copacabana*? Yes, I know, "Lola the Showgirl;" no matter what time period you look at, you'll see a "Lola" at a club, bar, or restaurant. Lola's that woman who hasn't developed her worth more than her utility and she lives a very, very sad existence.

Fucking Master: Absolutely. And, the male version of that is the old man at the bar or the club, and everybody knows him!

Trinity: Everybody knows them, and they look so desperate. They know time's closing in on them and they don't know what to do. They've developed nothing else and what they've had is fading fast. So, I get what you're saying . . .

Fucking Master: So, I've convinced you? You're on my side now?

Trinity: I just wouldn't take that approach, but I understand your approach . . .

Fucking Master: So, Sam at Safeway--can we call him "useless" yet?

(Laughter)

Trinity: I get what you're saying and I look forward to *this* book!

Fucking Master: Actually, I think it should be a chapter in the book.

Trinity: So, what should we call it?

Fucking Master: How about *Lessons from the Fucking Master*?

Hearing, at most, requires only compliance from the individual; whereas, listening requires you to be changed.

Fucking Master

Shut the Fuck Up and Listen

Trinity: In relationships, and in any form of communication, we all understand the importance of speaking; it does seem to be the #1 most central part of the communication process. Then, there's listening, which seems to come a distant second. But I often hear from men and women that he or she "just doesn't listen." Well, how important is listening and what is listening? People say, "Well it's just being quiet. You just listen; you just don't talk!" I'd like to speak about listening. What's your take on listening?

Fucking Master: Before you can understand "listening" you need to, first, know what is *hearing.* Hearing is basically inactive participation. We don't really have to be engaged or truly focused in order to hear. At best, even when we do participate fully at hearing, it always falls far short to listening.

Hearing and listening require focus and attention; but this focus and attention apparently uses different parts of the brain. Hearing, at most, requires only compliance from the individual; whereas, listening requires you to be changed. In addition, you can still accomplish hearing whether there are internal or external noises around. With listening, there must be silence on all fronts; the less silence the less listening. We have to be silent in order to listen fully. Maybe that's why when you rearrange the letters of the word *listen* you can get *silent*. One cannot listen without being silent, one cannot learn without being silent. It's only through listening that we learn anything. You source learning when you're in a listening state. When you're truly listening, you learn, because we learn nothing while we're talking. That's how you take things in, and so the most profound thing to say about listening is that it's a key to learning. Without listening, no one learns.

Now how much time do we give to truly listening? Not hearing, but listening. How much attention do you give to listening and what does it involve? Well, number one, you have to be deeply silent. You have to silence the internal dialogue and chatter. It has to be cut down, if not completely quieted, in order to learn. Think about anything you've learned in school. You had to be listening to have learned it, to have received it from the teacher.

To understand your mate and what they're feeling and what they're going through you have to be listening in order to understand what they're experiencing and what they're feeling.

Trinity: Well, I didn't actually have that distinction in school; hence, I heard the teachers but didn't learn much!

Fucking Master: Well, children aren't taught how to listen or the importance of listening.

Trinity: My point, exactly!

Fucking Master: Listening allows you to have experiences. When you're hearing, you're not experiencing much; you're still partly in your own head. You're thinking about, maybe, what you're doing later, or what you did yesterday. Listening, conversely, keeps you in the present; listening can only be done in the present. And, it's only in the present that you're actually able to experience something; something new. Therefore, we can say that listening allows you to experience the new. The deeper you can listen the more profoundly you can connect to life; the more profoundly you connect to life, the deeper your experiences will be. And with every experience we get the opportunity to change and grow. True listening will always change the listener.

Trinity: Well that has me really thinking about hearing. Before I could get listening, I had to listen to how I heard things.

Fucking Master: That's a great point!

Trinity: I would listen to something, but I would hear it from how I *already knew it to be.*

Fucking Master: That's the biggest problem, or one of the biggest blocks, that keeps us from truly being able to listen: our preconceptions and filters.

That's why practices like meditation, yoga, and reflecting, for example, enhance your ability to listen. When you engage in these practices, you become better equipped to keeping still . . . being quiet. When I describe meditation to people I, basically, say it's just the practice of going really, really quiet until you're fully silent and listening, and it's in that listening that you learn. It's in the listening that you get the information. It's in the listening that you can have the experience of the other, and the experience of what is actually going on around you.

SO the more silent I am, the more I can listen . . .

The more I can listen, the deeper I'm going to experience others . . .

The deeper I experience others; the better able I'll be in understanding what they're communicating . . .

The better I get their communication . . .

The greater I can connect with humanity.

This depth of connection is what will allow you to get other people's communication fully, and when I say fully, I mean all communications, both verbal and non verbal.

In our line of work, which is the study of Human Communication, it is said that 93% of all human communication is nonverbal; NONVERBAL. You get that? Just hearing what the other is saying is nowhere near enough. Therefore, you'll need to employ full listening in order to achieve enough connectedness with the other, so you'll be able to receive all the additional nonverbal communication. You'll need to listen . . . and that's not easy to do.

Trinity: I'm beginning to see that listening will require the use of *all my senses*.

Fucking Master: Yes. Even though listening is usually associated with the ears, the auditory system; it's really a state of being that includes the participation of all five of your senses. At any given moment, if you're attempting to receive full authentic communication, you'll need to engage all or some of these senses.

Trinity: Could you give me an example on how that would look?

Fucking Master: Sure. You could touch the other or notice if they touch you while they're speaking. You could notice the smells that surround you and the speaker; smells that may be influencing how the speaker is experiencing what she's talking about. You can observe his facial inflections and listen to her intonations, which may betray the speaker's hidden intention. Or, you could even imagine the" bad taste" a situation has left in their mouths.

In meditation, you go still and quiet and it's in this quiet that all five senses are enhanced. It's in this heightened state of awareness that you are able to access much more information than normal. With consistent practice you become quieter, thus more able to listen; thus you become a faster learner and you're able to get things done in a shorter period of time. But, if you're busy chattering, if you're busy using fillers, if you're busy in the past or the future, well . . . you're not going to be able to go silent enough to listen. So in other words, no education or learning can occur without listening; no listening occurs without silence.

Outside a school situation, most people believe they learn through conversation. Conversations, which usually include limited listening. Now, this is not because you don't necessarily *want* to listen but because you don't know exactly *how* to listen.

When I'm in a conversation, I say what I have to say and then I stop and fully go empty. I go silent so I can hear, then listen to what you have to say. Then I absorb what was said and can then communicate, in return. This process can get faster with time because the better you get at it the quicker you'll be with deciphering cues and signals. The more proficient you become at silencing your mind, the deeper you will listen, and the clearer and faster you'll get the communication. This creates a faster pace of learning, if needed.

But, if you're trying to tell me something before you've gotten my communication, you're not going to be able to listen to me. If you're trying to "tell me," or make a point, or convince me, without being interested, or encountering what I have to say . . . then you're going to be hearing me, you're not going to be listening to me. So, listening is probably one of the most profound skills one can acquire. It is the key that gets us through the door to **all** knowledge.

Trinity: Would you say we're having watered down conversations when we are just hearing one another?

Fucking Master: Well, yes; they're conversations that are filtered and obscured. They interfere with knowledge. It's watered down, as you said, or blocked by your preconceptions. How you're hearing something can distort the message. So, you think you're getting the other but what you're really getting is what you want to get. You're hearing what you want to hear. Please understand, I'm not saying preconceptions are wrong, like stereotypes; we need them to make sense of the world. The problem occurs when we become *frozen* in these preconceptions; when there is no flexibility to conceive of something new.

When you lack the skills to listen, you could be speaking to the most intelligent person in the world, who could teach you all sorts of things, but you're not going to learn anything because you don't know how to listen. You've trained yourself on only how to hear; so many of us have trained ourselves on hearing alone. Let's take a look at how you hear.

What are things that block your listening? Let's start with you, Danette; how do you hear a guy that is attractive?

Danette: Ummm . . . it's my thoughts of him. As he's talking I could see that I'd be creating scenarios of him and me in my head.

Fucking Master: Right, such as?

Danette: Depends . . . it's different; it depends on the person . . .

Fucking Master: It's not different. We're talking about a guy who's attractive . . . and you're single. It's going to be the same each time. What is it?

Danette: I'm looking for compatibility, or whether we can be mates.

Fucking Master: Exactly! Right . . . you're already hearing from, "Will this fit into what I'm looking for?" You're not listening to the guy . . . he might be telling you he's not interested. Or he might be telling you the very thing that warns you, "I should head for the hills!" But you're going to miss it, because you come from a preconceived wanting to hear what you want to hear to see if you can have a relationship . . . so the need for a relationship, affects your ability to listen.

Okay, Trinity, your turn. Let's look at you in a job interview? How much do you listen to the person interviewing you?

Trinity: Oh, not much!

Fucking Master: What *causes* your hearing in this situation?

Trinity: All I'm listening for is cues. I'm trying to figure out what they want me to say.

Fucking Master: So all you're *hearing* for are cues, so that you can convince them of something--to get them to approve of you; to hire you.

Trinity: Right.

Fucking Master: Then know you'll probably do most of the talking. You'll be busy trying to convince them to hire you. But if you're listening to the interviewer, and I've done this before, they'll wind up doing most of the talking. Because I'm listening intently to them, they wind up really liking me!

Trinity: I bet! That probably gets you the job on the spot!

Fucking Master: Oh, it's worked, I've done it.

Trinity: Wish I knew you a few years ago . . .

Shut the Fuck Up and Listen

(Laughter)

Fucking Master: You did . . . You just didn't listen!

(More Laughter)

Trinity: I'm talking twenty years ago . . . I've been self-employed for a long time. But I remember going on interviews, or auditions, when I was a singer/actress, and I did the same thing as you've just explained. I really didn't listen; I talked a lot without checking, "Do I even want this job?"

Fucking Master: I get it. You went into it in "hearing mode." You were already preset; you knew what you needed and wanted to hear. You already knew what you wanted to do.

Trinity: Yes, I was strictly looking for validation from what might have been an absolute witch or bastard! Actually, I remember one job, where I didn't listen during the interview. The director turned out to be an absolute ass. Looking back, it was clear in the interview what an ass he was, but I didn't find out until two months into the job.

Fucking Master: I've interviewed hundreds of people; . . . and what you mostly get is a series of stock answers; it's incredibly monotonous. You get these young people saying, "I'm enthusiastic . . . I'm a hard-worker . . . I'm excited . . . and, I have a lot to offer your company." These were stock answers to some very open questions I had come up with. Yes, I had some stock questions but I always tried to mix them up with *real* questions. Unfortunately, they came in with their pre-practiced preconceived answers, which caused me to, at least, hesitate in considering them. I'm not saying one shouldn't prepare for an interview. All I'm saying is you need to listen to what the moment calls for.

Trinity: So you didn't even need to be there, they could have sent in a tape.

Fucking Master: Exactly. The purpose of an interview is to be able to share and express what you haven't been able to communicate in your resume, and many people don't take advantage of that.

They may not be listening to my question, or listening to the room they're in, or listening to the pictures that I have on my table, and the type of person I might be or my feedback to them. They're not really present in the moment at all; they come rehearsed so it becomes . . . a play. It's not alive; it's a play, so there's a lot of hearing and performing going on with no real listening.

If the interviewer's aware, you're in trouble; you're not getting that job. Unless they see some potential in you and they ask a few questions that throw you off and throw you off your script. Then they can find something authentic in you. But if you're going to a job interview because you need the job and you need the money, you're going to be less inclined to listen. Alternately, if you're going for the job for creative purposes, if you want growth and you want possibility, you're more likely to be inclined to listen.

Shut the Fuck Up and Listen

Listening and the ability to listen are affected by where you're approaching your life from. If you are looking for the new or creative, it will be easier to listen; but, if you're tight, afraid, or in need, you will have more trouble listening.

So, Danette, let's say you're in a happy and fulfilling relationship and you meet an attractive guy . . . and he starts talking to you . . . do you think you're going to be listening or hearing him?

Danette: Listening.

Fucking Master: Right, you see your needs really dilute your ability to listen. If you're not conscious of your needs and how they're affecting you, then they are going to affect your listening; they're going to affect your ability to listen and learn.

So guess what? When you're highly needy in life, how much are you able to learn?

Danette: Very little.

Fucking Master: Yeah, do you get that? When you've been placed or have placed yourself in an exceptionally needy position, you will have less access to your ability to listen, which, in turn, limits your access to real information. But, if you've practiced listening till it's become a habit, you'll be able to access information under any circumstance. On the contrary, if you go unpracticed, you might get your needs met but you're not going to get any of the bonuses of knowledge, and definitely not wisdom. **So** listening is a key to knowledge, and knowledge with experience brings wisdom.

Understand that knowledge, by itself, without experience, is just that: knowledge. It's something that you read in a book, it's not something that arises from your depths. But if you have knowledge that is now linked with an authentic experience, you'll acquire wisdom. This is not possible without the ability to listen, because listening is what creates the experience, the ability to have the experience, so listening is the key to experiencing life!

Trinity: Because it is a full body experience!

Fucking Master: Exactly. It is a full body experience . . . well put. I wish I had said that!

(Laughter)

Trinity: Well you know . . . genius can't come to all of us!

(More laughter)

Trinity: In all seriousness, I have been the most profoundly moved in my life when I've truly listened, and that is because it was a full body experience.

Fucking Master: Absolutely.

Danette: I've had situations like that, too; where, when I've really listened, it's moved me on a totally different level. I've also had experiences where I would listen and people, who are normally used to somebody hearing and just responding quickly, would end up going on and on revealing so much more than they realized they were. I'm like "Oh my God, this person just keeps going and going, revealing and revealing." All I did was stop and I wouldn't talk, just to watch how far they would go.

Fucking Master: Good example; it makes the point. You went silent and were instantly educated about them. They gave you more than they had even planned to give.

Danette: Exactly.

Fucking Master: If you can go silent enough, you'll get all the information you'll ever need; most people can't help themselves. Again, like you said, if they're expecting hearing, it's going to throw them and they're going to start spilling their beans. Beans that could never be collected by hearing but which are easily scooped up, and even made into a bean stew, through listening!

Some of us think that listening is impolite. In other words, too much listening with too much thoughtfulness, might make someone uncomfortable, so "I'm not going to listen too deeply because I don't want them to be uncomfortable." Haven't you caught yourself doing that at times?

Danette: Yeah . . .

Fucking Master: So, we actually limit ourselves that way; which is ridiculous, because their discomfort shouldn't be our concern.

Shut the Fuck Up and Listen

I once had an ex-girlfriend who accused me of listening too well. I had repeated, with insight, what she had said and her response was "My God, you listen to everything!" She did not mean it as a compliment.

(Laughter)

This confused me because I thought at the time "Isn't this what women complain that men don't do enough of?" In truth, most people--**not just** women--aren't really looking for listeners; they're looking for *hearers*.

In my experience, most women weren't looking for me to listen to them; they wanted me to just hear them. They wanted me to hear their stories, and their gossip and their complaints. They wanted me to *hear* about that "bitch" they worked with that's pissed them off. They didn't want me to listen; they wanted me to hear, only.

Are women, in fact, really interested in men who listen or men who hear? I think that's an interesting question. I would look forward to an argument on that at a future date.

Trinity: Yeah, that is going to be a future date and we will argue about that one, because there's some more points to that, that I don't want to go into now, because there are people listening . . .

(Laughter)

Fucking Master: Well if I can at least end this by saying I hope you'll understand that when, in the future, I tell you to **shut the fuck up and listen**, that I'm actually being kind in asking you to do something that's useful for you . . . to help you listen.

(Laughter)

Trinity: You are so rude and crude! Anyways, this was a good conversation!

Fucking Master: Once again, she has to approve; she has to approve every conversation!

(Laughter)

You can't be human by selecting; you can only be human by exploring.

Fucking Master

Are You Likeable?

Alice is a 40-something year old yoga instructor, on the verge of a divorce.

(Alice calls, crying)

Fucking Master: Good morning, sweetheart. How are you doing?

Alice: Not well. I'm calling as a friend who needs a friend to talk to.

Fucking Master: Okay, then, let's get right to it. What is it you are feeling?

Alice: Um . . . most of the time?

Fucking Master: Right now.

Alice: Right now? Embarrassed.

Fucking Master: Okay, so if Embarrassment's a spirit what do you think it wants from you?

Alice: To be honest.

Fucking Master: What else does Embarrassment want from you?

Alice: To feel.

Fucking Master: Right!

Alice: Instead of do . . . I just feel like all I've done is work, work, work and do and stay busy. I just keep going, to prove that I can do it and I'm so tired, and I can't do it. I feel defeated. I feel that I just needed to prove that I could do it. I have felt so much resentment and anger and now all

I feel is just . . . I wake up in the middle of the night screaming.

Fucking Master: Sounds . . . like you feel cornered.

Alice: Yes, and then put into a box. I've allowed myself to go in there. I was aware of going in there and then that door was shut and the top got closed and I don't know how to get out.

Fucking Master: Who put you in the box?

Alice: I don't know?

Fucking Master: Have you ever been out of it?

Alice: No, never . . .

Fucking Master: But, you just said you were aware of going in it.

Alice: I guess I was aware when the top came down on me.

Fucking Master: So, someone or something put you in there and you don't remember who did this or when this happened.

Alice: No.

Fucking Master: So, how do you imagine you got in there?

(Long silence)

Yeah, you can't remember, because you've always been in it, you get it?

Are You Likeable?

You first have to come to understand that no one's placed you in it because you've always been in the box. It's a big difference to know you've always been in it. Then at least you know that you didn't make the mistake of going in through another or on your own. Furthermore, the frustration you're feeling is not meant to make you feel badly but rather have you awaken to the fact that you've been living in a box your whole life.

Do you consider yourself a likable person?

Alice: Sometimes.

Fucking Master: What makes you likable, sometimes?

Alice: My magnificent personality . . . (Sarcastic laughter)

Fucking Master: So what is it about your personality that makes you likable? What's magnificent about it? Be specific. I'm not disagreeing with you.

Alice: I try to give people what they want.

Fucking Master: That's not likable, keep going . . . what makes you likable? Trying to give people what they want is not likable. What's the energy like when someone *tries* to give you what you want?

Alice: Phony.

Fucking Master: Yeah, you can feel it, it's like "get the fuck away from me" . . . right? So tell me what about your personality makes you likable?

Are You Likeable?

Alice: I think I'm fun.

Fucking Master: Okay, that's a little closer . . . so you bring fun? You bring to people, fun?

Alice: No. I think I bring to people a freedom . . .

Fucking Master: Okay. So, tell me more about that.

Alice: I think I'm likable to a lot of people because I allow them to be who they are.

Fucking Master: Now we're getting even closer. How do you do that?

Alice: I try really hard not to judge them. Because there's a big part of me that just has an understanding of what people go through.

Fucking Master: So, there's a big part of you that understands what people go through, so it makes it un-judge-able on your end, right?

Alice: Yes.

Fucking Master: You don't try *not* to judge, it's un-judge-able isn't it? Even if you tried to judge, you couldn't, right?

Alice: Uh hmm.

Fucking Master: So you allow people to be as they are and in that moment they feel a freedom.

Alice: Yeah, I think so.

Fucking Master: I don't want you to think about it, I want you to know this because it's time you know this. You need to feel it, not think it.

Now, put yourself in the receiving position. Let's say you are sitting with a woman who's been through a lot in life and has handled it and grown from it through doing self work. Let's say she's practiced and utilized Yoga, meditation, and contemplation and because of these practices she's neutralized judgment, she's now un-judge-able. How would you feel in her presence? How would you feel when you're sharing your pains with her?

Alice: Accepted.

Fucking Master: And in that acceptance are you left feeling some degree of freedom?

Alice: Yes.

Fucking Master: So, with a person like yourself, you would feel some freedom. With a person like yourself, you'd feel accepted. Even if you don't feel full freedom you'd feel acceptance from this woman, right?

Alice: Hmm.

Fucking Master: Okay. So, you tell me? Do you think or do you *know* that you help people feel accepted and/or free even if it's for a moment.

Alice: Yeah, I know that.

Are You Likeable?

Fucking Master: Okay, it's time to know that this is part of what makes you likable. Why does it make you likable?

Alice: Because I am.

Fucking Master: No, why does it make you likable, able to be liked, likeable? What makes you able to be "liked," in that moment?

Alice: Because I like me?

Fucking Master: No. That would make you unlikable.

Alice: (Laughter) . . . I don't know.

Fucking Master: Because you suddenly become like them, you understand them, you empathize with them, you don't judge them, and you be with them and give them something. Whether it's the feeling of being accepted, or you give them the feeling of freedom, even if it's for a moment. In that moment, not only do you contribute to them, but you become like them. In order to understand them, you have to become like them and so you become likable! It's only when you are giving, in this way, are you likable; even if it's for a moment.

Now the problem is you've never seen that you were like anyone else. So, you live very isolated. Actually, you have become more *like* everyone else than you've realized. Do you think what you're saying and feeling right now is any different than what I hear three or four times a week from four or five different people a day? Your insistence of wanting to be un-like everyone else makes you unlikable to them and to yourself. Ultimately, doesn't this behavior leave you feeling invaluable, useless, unwanted, not needed . . . am I getting close? Sound familiar?

Alice: Yes.

Fucking Master: Now you tell me, where does your power to change this experience come from?

Alice: From understanding that I'm liked . . . that I'm not so different; that I'm even the same, in many ways.

Fucking Master: Exactly . . . we don't have to be the same in every way. But we have to know we are the same in most ways. Remember, if you try to **make** me like you, that's not being like me is it?

Alice: No.

Fucking Master: If you say the right things or wear the right clothes are you being like me?

Alice: No.

Fucking Master: No, because that's external. Do you understand? Copying and mimicking is external; it's the realm of the personality, the Ego. Sameness is internal. When you're in your center, you are the most human; it is where humanity begins. It's the place in all of us where we can meet and it's in that place that we're all the same: human. When you're in your sameness, even the personality is vulnerable to liking you. This is not to say all people will like you, for some are pure surface, never reaching, nor wanting to reach their center. They won't like you because you'd be "too human."

What you need to understand more than anything is, because of your practices, you **are** deeply human! You have spent so much time in your humanity that you don't need to work as hard. You no longer need to confine yourself in the box in order to fit in and be accepted. All you have to do is be **you** and people will like you, thus accept you just as you are.

So, right now, talking to you, you're likable. There are times, when you call, that you're fucking unlikable. It's when you've bought into the external nonsense, and for me, it's like 'Oh my God, now I have to deal with all this bullshit!'

You don't have to jump through hoops to find commonality with others. When you're centered in your humanity, it is effortless to connect and give. It becomes easier for you to *see* other humans. Hence, whatever you give is profound because of where it's sourced. It might occur to you as minor gift what you give, but actually it creates warmth in the other that leaves them filled beyond even the most extravagant of gifts. This type of giving ultimately causes the receiver to follow. This is the process that creates a true leader; and it's very difficult to become a leader. To be a leader you must have first followed, and in your case you've done so inconsistently. You need to fully follow my leadership and your practices. What you've done instead is shun the position of leadership that is meant to be naturally yours, and foolishly followed the mass Ego.

Are You Likeable?

This external craving to fit in is degrading to you. Hopefully, before you die, you're going to look back at all this and laugh. I know your laugh and I'm going to hear it. You're going to laugh so hard at yourself when you see that you wanted to be like them, meanwhile you were them all along. It's like an ant saying I wish I was an ant. You're going to laugh so hard when you realize the irony and that, the whole time, it was you who actually created this gap and distance.

Alice: I've learned a lot since I've been out here. There's a big difference in the life I lead. I love sitting down with these old cowboys. I love sitting down and listening to their stories. There's this one particular old man who had a stroke who has loved horses his whole life and I guess that's our common line. He's learned to trust me; everybody else pays no attention to him. I sit down and chat with him and I find that I spend more time with people now than I ever have. I realized so much of my past was just living in this illusion, this is really hard to say, but I felt . . . like I was fucking pretentious. I felt like I was above it. I lost track of the common folk. What does that mean? You know, like, I'm something different. But living out here on the ranch and having to spend . . . not having too . . . but *electing* to spend the time alone to integrate, I realized I do enjoy people more than I ever have. I'm not as guarded as I used to be, I don't have to be something and I don't have to pretend! I just engage in conversations and I talk to them about what their interests are and I learn from them. I realize that when I was younger I made up they were something simple.

Are You Likeable?

Fucking Master: If I wake up in the morning and I don't eat any breakfast, and I'm sluggish at noon, and I go "Why the fuck am I sluggish at noon." Then I wake up the next day and I don't eat breakfast and I'm sluggish at noon, and I go, "Why am I sluggish at noon?" Then I wake up the next day and I eat breakfast and I'm wide awake at noon, and I go "Wow! Why am I wide awake today?" Then I wake up the next day and eat breakfast and I'm full of energy at noon and I say again "Why am I full of energy at noon," and finally if I go to wake up the next day and I don't eat breakfast and I'm sluggish at noon and I go, "Why am I sluggish at noon?" Well then I'm just a fucking dumbass.

If I see what works and I don't do it, what other result should I expect? You know how to do this; you know how to be like other human beings. So why aren't you going to your humanity? Why are you dabbling in the realm of the personality? Why are you intentionally diminishing yourself?

You want to know that it's very telling who you are choosing to be human with. Old cowboys, older men, these are clearly father figures with whom you feel safe, who you trust. But, why limit the world to one type. There are many other types: daughters, sons, cousins, aunts, uncles, boyfriends, husbands, girlfriends, and acquaintances and nurses and doctors. Why just old cowboys; why just older men? Why identify with only older men? You don't have balls like them, you don't have a cock like them, and you don't have much that's the same, physically, as them. Why aren't you including everyone else?

Are You Likeable?

Alice: I do, though. I do include other people. I give my time and have allowed so many more people into my life.

Fucking Master: And what is it like in those moments . . . when you've had your breakfast?

Alice: It feels really good.

Fucking Master: There we go. So, when you don't feel good you find yourself not *liked* and when you do feel good you're liked. You think it's because of your feelings that you're liked or not but, in actuality, it's about whether or not you've had your *breakfast*. You wonder, "Why do I feel isolated, separate, and distanced" rather than meditating upon these feelings in order to uncover what is truly underneath them? Your wondering is self indulgent; it is focus-less. Again, there will be people who you don't like and who don't like you, and that's fine. Move on, don't waste any time with them. Move on; because with them, you have to pretend. Because they're not like anything; there's no substance to them. Now it's easy to be liked and likable when you're with people of substance. These old cowboys have found some substance in bowing to nature, haven't they? So they have substance. It's okay if you chose to be *like* people because you're able to *like*.

Let's take your neighbors wife. I've met her; I don't like her at all! She's not likable; she doesn't have the ability to be like anyone. She insists that she's different, because she was adopted; she insists that she's so different and separate from everyone because she was "rejected by her parents." That perspective has helped her become completely unlikable. She can't meet you in a likable manner, and the only place that she experiences any connection in her life, is from her children because they're the only ones who won't reject her. So, she tries to be like them instead and now she's an adult with a child's mind wreaking havoc in her life. Now, does any of this sound familiar?

Alice: Oh, absolutely. That's me with all my animals.

Fucking Master: Right . . . now the animals are meant to be a transition for you to return you to being human. It's very difficult to remember to be human once we've wandered far into the external world.

Alice: Especially since I live in a zoo! (Laughter)

Fucking Master: Hey listen, you're preaching to the choir! I lived across the street from the Bronx Zoo for eight years. I understand this; I lived it too. And since it was located in a tough part of the Bronx, then you could say I was surrounded by animals on all ends.

(Laughter)

So, it's difficult to be human in all of that! But animals are a great practice to help us return to humanity. We can't stop there, though. Since you've recently extended yourself with others, outside your box, you may want to also allow yourself to receive.

When we are in *likeness,* we, too, can be gifted. Be open to the fact that in the space of *likeness*, you can receive that which you crave and need the most. Don't underestimate

Are You Likeable?

what you can get from transacting with others in that place. It's a gift, that when received, leaves us with feelings of joy and gratitude that are contagious. These gifts are experiences that become a part of us. At that point, in those moments, we know the truth! In those moments, we know that we're interdependent with one another, or more precisely, inter-independent with one another. That's a beautiful moment! But we have to make that happen through participation within.

The first thing my mind does when confronted with an idea is to rip it apart in order to make sense of it. Therefore, I have to make an additional effort to look at it wholly, from a different angle, and put it back together. If I didn't, I'd become a cynical, critical individual, always tearing things apart including those around me. So even at my age I still have to make an effort to stop and look at things on a wide scale. You have to do the same. You have to make an effort to see and be in what is LIKE each other, to look for what's alike and be in it. Then, you'll have the opportunity, once you do that, to GIVE! Presently, you do it randomly, accidently, like my breakfast story. I promise you the same result . . . every time . . . if you make this effort. The feelings of isolation will diminish! But you have to make an effort to find the likeness of being with others. Of course, it's easier for you to do it with someone who has stability and who doesn't put any pressure on you, like me. That's why you need to do it because **you** want it, not because others require it or anything like that. Now are you likeable to your son?

Alice: Yes.

Fucking Master: Why? You should be able to explain it to me now.

Alice: When I'm with him, it's effortless, I don't feel that I have to be anything but who I am, and it comes from a place of love and acceptance.

Fucking Master: Who causes that experience and result?

Alice: Me.

Fucking Master: You get it; 100% do you get it? Do you put it on him? Do you rely on him to create it?

Alice: No, I don't.

Fucking Master: Why was it that, when you first called, you specified that you wanted to talk to me as a friend rather than the teacher?

Alice: I don't know. I just wanted to talk to a friend . . .

Fucking Master: Why? What's so special about a friend?

Alice: I feel . . .

Fucking Master: Don't feel, think! That will take us an hour, I don't want you feeling, don't hurt yourself.

(Laughter)

Alice: It's safe.

Fucking Master: Why?

Are You Likeable?

Alice: It's so hard when you say "don't feel" because all I want to talk about is my feelings when I'm upset. I want to focus on everything I feel.

Fucking Master: Okay if you want to feel, touch your clit. That way, you can talk to me about why you want to talk to your friend; that way you can distract your feelings.

(Laughter)

Cut it out with the fuckin' feelings. What do you think? Just your intelligence; what do you think?

Alice: I think it's easier.

Fucking Master: Right, why?

What happens with a friend; let's say, your best friend?

Alice: There's love and acceptance from her, she brings joy to the conversation; I trust her.

Fucking Master: Right. Okay, so let's talk about the elephant in the room. How about the likability factor?

Alice: What about it?

Fucking Master: You don't have to feel; give me just your thoughts.

Alice: Well, we're alike.

Fucking Master: Exactly

Alice: It's comfortable; I stay in my comfort zone.

Are You Likeable?

Fucking Master: It's not so much about your comfort zone. It's just that you want to meet in likability and that's when you actually expand the box. You see, what you forget is that our boxes are expandable because we live in an infinite space so the only way not to fly off or just wander around in space is to create a box to live through. The box has a great purpose. We can go in and out of that box through things like meditation, or sex, but basically, we like staying in the box; we can expand it. Your box is too tight.

When you're in the state of finding a likeness with others you automatically start expanding your box, you have to know this. When you said "I want to talk to my friend," you were saying I want to speak to someone that's LIKE me and that I'm LIKE. When you call your best friend, you create the possibility of her providing you joy and you have the possibility of providing her acceptance and freedom. That's what you wanted . . . that's what you meant when you said I want to talk to my friend. You wanted the thing you're craving, and so, with your son, you don't wait to crave it, you create it. With a friend you don't reach for enough, you wait to crave it, instead of creating it. Now why do you treat your son or children or animals different than adults? Because it doesn't make a difference.

Alice: Okay . . .

Fucking Master: Okay what? What do you get from that?

Alice: That my sense of my aloneness is completely self-created, and it's a choice. It's not something that's been put on me . . .

Fucking Master: Bravo! (Clapping)

Alice: Nobody has abused me or abandoned me. Those things have been coming up for me when I'm dreaming. All I've been dreaming of is when my dad was dying.

Before last year all I remembered of him was when he was alive and healthy and now . . . all I remember is when he was dying and really thin, he was like 80 pounds. I slept beside his bed. He really didn't appear human to me. I keep having a memory of him like that; it really scares me!

Fucking Master: What this reveals is that your parent's were the only humans you allowed yourself to connect with. They were the only ones who you went in with and found like-ability. Most of us do that, and that is why we cling to them like they're the only source. It's like me sleeping next to a kitchen water faucet because I'm scared I'll never have water again. Meanwhile, if I just walked to the bathroom, there I'd find another water faucet. But I don't do that, I cling to the kitchen water faucet. I set up a mat, a couch, a bed, in the kitchen. This is kind of what you did because you insisted that connectedness could only come through them. What the dream was trying to tell you was "It's time to grow up, little girl. Let go of your parents; there are other people you can drink from, and who can drink from you . . ."

Alice: Is that what I did with my husband, also?

Fucking Master: Yes, that's what you do with anyone you can latch on to that you feel is family. Because they're family you give yourself permission to try to possess; with non family you don't even ask! You don't connect, you don't attach, too.

Alice: No, like even when I phoned my friend I felt like I was bothering her.

Fucking Master: Yeah. Tell me something I don't already know. You only allow yourself to do this with family. You don't understand that these other humans are also family. Science has proved it; genetics connect us all. This *family* distinction is a creation of your own mind, it doesn't exist in reality. Have you ever called your friend, family? I'm sure you have. This happens to you in moments you drop into your center, or in moments of clarity when you're with animals, or even when you're teaching yoga. It's in all those moments that you are able to experience a sense of family with anyone. When you are teaching yoga it becomes even easier for you to experience oneness. You facilitate the connecting and you do this by first dropping into your own center. You use yoga to create simple connections because yoga's all about simple connections isn't it? From one movement to another, always in a rhythm that creates a likeness. Your only limitation as a teacher is that you do it physically, a bit mentally, but you refuse to do it emotionally because you cling to your parents. Now, when your father was dying you were becoming nothing like him. The closer someone gets to death the less we become like them, why? We start losing that connection, why?

Alice: Because we're separating.

Are You Likeable?

Fucking Master: Yes, why are we becoming less like them as a person starts to die?

Alice: Because we have life and they don't.

Fucking Master: Close enough. I'll check with the judges, the judges approve. Okay.

Alice: I went to a place of breath while I was with him, without breath you're in a different realm, you're somewhere else, and there is a disconnection from my experience.

Fucking Master: The answer's easy . . . they're becoming less human. They're becoming less human so there's no likeness. As they begin to die, as I begin to die one day, I will become less human and the closer I get to it the less people will connect with me.

You're still trying to drink from your father's faucet even when you're engaging with old cowboys. You need to let go of primarily connecting with his human likeness because you're missing out on the twofold gift that comes with new connections. Gift number one is experienced when we've connected with another and we feel a sudden *likeness* with them; we see ourselves in them. The second gift is in when we experience a likeness of them in us.

Presently, there's nothing but grief and emptiness in your second hand encountering. All you're doing is revisiting a grave where there's an empty body. It's a one-fold gift with the old cowboy because all that's experienced is you get to see you in him. Don't fool yourself, you're not really seeing him fully; it's tainted by your image of father.

Alice: What do I do then, about my father?

Fucking Master: He had to leave the human likeness you shared together. Now he's in the spiritual realm, so you can find a spiritual likeness with him now; especially since you've established a *human* connection. We can have a spiritual likeness with those who've departed because it is in spirit that **all** is connected. The problem here is, as humans, we try to connect spiritually before we connect humanly. That never works! What do I mean by that? We're supposed to connect humanly and then our *human-ness* gets lifted and connected where we ultimately bond in spirit. This applies whether you're dealing with someone who's alive or dead.

Alice: Hmm, so true connection is only possible through likeness.

Fucking Master: Yes. It's by connecting our human natures that we find a likeness. This likeness eradicates loneliness and isolation. But this takes action on your part.

Unfortunately, we confuse action with attraction. We tend to move towards only the things and people that are familiar to us, *family-like*. This attraction is not action. It's just comfort or laziness. Furthermore, the problem with being with only that which attracts us is that, then, we become vulnerable to projecting anything that is family upon the new object, thus, never knowing the object at hand. We project mother or father on mate or spouse. It takes an action of stepping out of what's *family-like* to find true like-ness. This is why people, who have never stepped out of what's familiar, live with subtle or blatant feelings of isolation and loneliness. It is when we connect with what is unfamiliar, on a human level, that we establish a bond that causes spirit to come forth. A bond that is permanent and eternal. When we do it with only what's familiar or safe we don't fully bond with all of humanity, just a part of it and that is not enough to transcend the separateness we all experience when we come into this world. I was able to figure this out experientially; through much trial and error.

My family system wasn't very supportive, so I turned to another *familiar* option in sex and drugs. Every time I took a drug, I experienced a spiritual connection. Every time I had sex I experienced a spiritual connection. I used sex. Sex was like drugs and drugs were like sex to me. In both cases I avoided real human contact. I cheated. I became lazy and kept doing these things instead of doing it in a natural way; instead of connecting through humanity and then to spirit. If I had done that, then I'd own my spiritual connection. Instead I used to just rent it and, eventually, this approach tore me apart; all the king's horses and all the king's men couldn't put this Humpty together again. So, I had to start from scratch.

Alice: Yeah I think I've rented to own, I think I might have paid off everything by now.

Fucking Master: You see? You do have ability now. If you want to be human for whatever little time you have left. You don't have much though . . . none of us have much time left. You're already in your fifth decade . . . how many more do you think you have left here? When would you like to be human?

Alice: Right now.

Fucking Master: When would you like to connect with us and be like us? It's in our likeness that we become likable, and as we feel likable and be likable, the other feels the same and as they become likable we have a mutual orgasm; in other words we exchange our gifts. Imagine trying to have an orgasm without any touching, no penetration, and no conversation? You can't, unless you're in a dream. Why haven't you had an orgasm?

With sexuality we wait for the body to get lubricated and aroused; it takes some time. You talk or you touch until you have a deeper connection and with some movement, you might have this spiritual experience called an orgasm. Sex teaches us how to do it! We don't listen to it; we use it instead. If we followed Sex we'd learn how to connect and find our humanity. If we encountered others as Sex intended us to, we'd sit and be with them, we'd connect, we'd listen, we'd hear, and we'd get to feel out and see if there's some likeness. If there weren't, we'd move on. If there was, we'd explore it and we'd feel likable and the other would be likable to you. At this point, full human connection occurs which leads to orgasm. How would this look from the outside looking in? Well, what you'd see is a physical synchronicity, orgasmic laughter and warmth with affection. This is how you feel when you bond with your friend who brings joy, isn't it?

Alice: Yes!

Fucking Master: She brings joy, you provide freedom, and you both burst into full, mutual orgasms.

Alice: I want to have more!

Fucking Master: So, what I've been trying to say to you all along is that you're basically a dead fuck. (Laughter)

Alice: No one's ever called me that, but hey, alright!

Fucking Master: Yeah, but when it comes to being human, you're a dead fuck, do you get it?!

Alice: Yes. (Laughter)

Fucking Master: Actually, if you're not a dead fuck in sex then you should be ashamed that you're not using it in your being humanness.

Alice: I do get that! You know what I am? I'm still too selective. There's so much ego and bullshit that gets in the way . . .

Fucking Master: You can't be human by selecting; you can only be human by exploring.

Alice: I get that from what you were saying, I really understand it the way you explained it to me.

Fucking Master: You're not trying to be human by selecting. That's something else. That's another play of the game. When we are selective we are being more like androids, robots, and machines.

Alice: Hence, my suffering?

Fucking Master: Yes, that's because robots and machines are for utility.

Alice: Hmm.

Fucking Master: So, the utility you're seeking is safety; that's why you're being selective. You're not being human!

Alice: But still, at any time, I can walk away, right? If I don't feel a likeness, I don't have to be engaged further.

Fucking Master: No, you don't.

Alice: I was being likable in a fraudulent way in my youth because I had to be like everyone and give them what they wanted because I needed them to love me.

Fucking Master: Excellent. Let me give you an example. I want you to put yourself back in grade 10; you're walking around the high school and you start talking and trying to find a likeness with others and, after a while, you realize there's no likeness to be found. At this point what you probably did was figure out what you needed to **do** to engage, to be nice, cordial, and included. You looked to see what they wanted and you gave it to them without questioning, if that was what you wanted to give. But what if you had walked away, what ripple effect would that have had on your present day? I'm saying right now, let's say it happened and you just abruptly walked away. What would your life look like today? What effect would it have had?

Alice: I don't know . . .

Fucking Master: Zero. It would have had no effect. If you stayed to be nice, that made no fucking difference because you were being and dealing with robots. If you're dealing with a robot, it makes no difference. It's better to cut your losses and move on! It's not going to make a difference in your life. The only thing that makes a difference is when we hurt people who are connected to something human. There are people you just can't hurt. They're so disconnected. If you examine what is on TV today, you'd notice there's a huge disconnection for many of the youth. They can watch someone slam against a door fall down and hurt themselves badly and they'll laugh their heads off. This is becoming an epidemic. The world needs a "You" and a "Me," to remind itself how to connect, how to be human. We are forgetting how to be human.

Alice: Is the rage that I feel right now coming from the belief I've held that I was abandoned and have blamed others for leaving me? When, in fact, it was me who kicked their asses out the door?

Fucking Master: Yes.

Alice: I feel so angry right now. It's beyond anger; the last few weeks have just been a rage.

Fucking Master: Okay, let me ask you a question. If you're human and you're being human, can anybody leave you?

Are You Likeable?

Alice: No.

Fucking Master: No. It's when a person becomes non-human that they've left . . . themselves. You left yourself before your father died and now you're raging at life, or him, for your loneliness. This loneliness was not caused by his passing.

Alice: Okay. It's my attachment. Its how I attach to a very few people and they become my whole world. And because they're my whole world when they walk out, when they're not there anymore, physically, or through death, I'm lost.

Fucking Master: What you need to see is that you use them to hide your feelings of being lost, instead of *likening* yourself with them. If you had connected with them fully on a human level, you would have naturally included more and more people to your pool. Connecting is contagious. What you did was use these people to hide your pain; it's what you call attaching, instead of linking with them to expand your humanity. At that point they were just faucets. So, what happens when our one or two faucets permanently stop working?

Alice: We'd be really thirsty.

Fucking Master: Yeah . . . you might start laying there and gasping for water, and people will have to come and bring you water and force feed you. That's how ridiculous we become. We don't go and get what we need. So, this is wonderful because this is linked to your father's passing. He had to eventually become not human as will you one day. You think your son should be pissed off at you once you become not human. What are you doing with your father and his passing? What would you want your son to do with you after you leave this body?

Alice: Continue loving me.

Fucking Master: And how would he connect with you?

Alice: Through experiences that we've had in this lifetime.

Fucking Master: Okay. That's the past. How else could he connect with you in the present? Where are you going to be?

Alice: I'll just be a spirit.

Fucking Master: Right, and so where would you want him to connect with you?

Alice: Spiritually.

Fucking Master: And wouldn't it be a shame if he kept connecting with you in past memories?

Alice: Yes it would.

Fucking Master: You know how many couples live together not connected in the present and spinning about their past memories together and only staying together because of their past memories?

Alice: Yes, I do.

Fucking Master: We all do. It's a shame we do that, it's silly, we have each other right here. To do it with someone that's alive is ridiculous. It's understandable when someone dies, then we have to make that switch from the physical to the spiritual.

You have to see that your father has been waiting; you have gone forward but he's waiting. As things stand now, he'll have to wait till you die before he can fully connect with you.

That's why you're dreaming so much, sweetie. It's because you're stuck in the past with him while he's waiting for you to complete the past so he can be with you spiritually. Dreams are the only avenue you're leaving available to him.

There have been times in the past when my spouse and I were having problems and she'd be connecting with me and it would be like "Okay! I'm not alone; I'm with likeness even though there's tension between us." Then, something would happen, maybe something frightening and she'd disconnect. Maybe it was a past memory of me which caused her to disconnect, or a past memory of her father that she saw in me. Suddenly, I'm alone, sitting around waiting for her to connect with me. I'd even go as far as beg or scream to get her real attention but to no avail. Like a telephone, she was disconnected. I might as well be a ghost screaming and yelling.

Now, It's her job to reconnect with her humanity, not mine, I can't force that upon another and you tried to force that upon your husband, for how long? He refused to! He was more selective than you! He made you look like a buyer at Costco. You buy bulk; he buys specific gourmet items.

We cannot force our partners to wake up and be present to us. But we can know what it's going to take for us to stay mutually human. It's very difficult to be human but when we're in our humanity we find likeness. When we find likeness then we become likable and once that happens both ways we've created a great back and forth rhythm of energy! You get your orgasm . . . and you feel free and filled with joy! It's that simple. But we have to make the self, not other, effort, just like you have to make the effort in sex, right?

Alice: Right.

Fucking Master: So, the real question here is why are you a dead fuck in life and not in sex? Because there's not a lot of time left on this planet and would you like to do the work? I'm being very specific with what the work looks like; it's not a vague term or action. It's spiritual work that begins through humanness; it's very specific. Would you like to do the work to become human? You don't have to select, but encounter and if you find nothing there you can move on. You can look at someone and say, "Oh, I'm talking to a vase, I need to move on." You don't have to worry about hurting their feelings or anything because they're a vase. You don't have a problem picking up a vase and putting it somewhere else without saying sorry and excuse me, do you? No, all you have to do is place it down, with care, and move on.

Are You Likeable?

My partner used to question me on how I could be so mean to people in our seminars. Well, that's easy if they're playing vases because they can't feel anything anyways, so I say shut up, stay in the penalty box, and then she'd be stunned that they wouldn't leave and they'd come back for more! What she's come to understand is what I'm doing in that moment is helping them snap out of it. I reject their personas and challenge their humanity to come forth.

We all want likability, or the ability to be liked, but it's not the likability of being accepted that I'm speaking about. Likability of acceptance is the approach of the EGO. It places the responsibility of feeling accepted upon others. This is proper when we are children but once we become adults, it's fucked!

You need to accept your human self because you're not going to be it for much longer. I had an experience in 2009 that I almost didn't come back alive from, and when I came back I said holy fuck, I don't want to waste another human moment, not being human. I want to be human. Previously, I spent my whole life chasing *being spiritual* and I almost succeeded! I nearly died. What the fuck was I doing!?

Alice: You know what? I really understand that! I was so lost in my search for the spiritual and all I found in the spiritual was a sense of disconnect from everyone else.

Fucking Master: Exactly. Because the only way you're going to feel the spiritual, in a connected fashion, is starting from your humanity.

Are You Likeable?

Alice: I feel that and it humbles me, and I KNOW that, more than feeling it, I know that. You know, my friend said something really poignant. She said "Are you trying to be Buddha or Jesus?" It's crazy

Fucking Master: I spent a little time trying to be a Buddhist, and I just wound up becoming a Bootyist. It just didn't work!

(Laughter)

If you just practice being human . . . if you just practice that, you'll have a different life for the rest of the time you're here, my love.

Because then you can observe yourself. Observe the experience that you're having! Then, there is not so much judgment and harshness on you. You know when you called and said I'm embarrassed . . . I know you have a story that follows that, like a confession, and if you can just have compassion for yourself, you'll have the freedom to be human and then make choices that are serving you.

How do you feel now?

Alice: I feel SO much better! I feel connected, not alone. I don't feel guilty.

Fucking Master: I want to hear what you do feel, not what you don't. How does it feel to not feel alone?

Are You Likeable?

Alice: There's peacefulness to it. I was feeling absolute agitation and now I feel calmness and I'm looking forward to being likable. Living!

Fucking Master: And now you are likable. In other words, you are able to like; to link with all of us or any of us that you choose. You can let go of the few faucets you link to. You're not imprisoned by them now. In addition, there's this little bonus awaiting you . . . it's your father who has been **waiting** for you to link to him, spiritually. You see, we try to do that with people while they're alive; it doesn't work. The only time you have permission to link directly to someone, spiritually, is in death. Not in life! How often do we try to do it in life and it's not till they're dead that we realize all we ever wanted was an authentic human moment, just one more human moment with them.

Alice: Ass backwards.

Fucking Master: No kidding!

It felt like an overwhelming pile of crap the size of a mountain in this grief and pain you've been feeling, but in reality it was the width of an inch. It was a mirage. You just have to work to see it.

Don't allow yourself to be a dead fuck in life, anymore. It will take effort, though. So what? I might have to take a pill every day for the rest of my life but, if it's going to keep me here, what's a pill a day?

The tension that you have is simply the agitation and rage you feel about not letting yourself **be** human. Do you get that? I want you to really listen to this! Your anger is at not letting yourself be human!

Alice: I went from trying to be what everyone wanted me to be and needed from me and then I flipped the coin and I thought I'm just so fucking tired of doing all this work to be approved of, I don't give a shit. Because I've been looking for acceptance from the elected few, I haven't been able to just enjoy life. The biggest thing for me today is, knowing that I can walk away! You see, I did walk away before, but there was a bitch connection to it. I really learned how to be a bitch, and just walk away, but there was still attachment to it. I loved the freedom when you offered that, to just look at it and just walk away! Without any attachment you can just simply walk away! It's such a feeling of relief.

Fucking Master: Again, you want to understand the source of your anger. That's the biggest part. Then you can give yourself permission to be human, and all that anger will drop because it's done its job; to awaken you to your abandonment of your humanity.

I was so hyper self-conscious in high school that I worried about everything I said. I thought if I said the wrong thing it would be remembered till the end of time. Of course, not one fucker there probably remembers even a word I spoke. Apparently, I wasn't as important as I thought I was.

Alice: I understand that, I can look back and remember thinking "I'm so important and everything I do, people will notice and I have to be aware of all of my actions", give me a break! There's accountability but then there's just pomposity that's based in bullshit, huge ego.

Fucking Master: I love that word! Pomposity! It sounds just like its meaning.

You say you're missing your ex-husband, even though you're having a relationship with a new man. What is that about? Why are you choosing to long for your ex, to live in the past? Why are you resisting connecting in the present? You now know enough to answer these questions.

Alice: The first thing that comes to me is the lack of me giving myself what I need. There's a desire for a man to give me what I need, to be there for me and create safety for me. When that comes up, the best thing for me to do is to connect with what **I'm** lacking? What am I not giving myself?

Fucking Master: Good. As long as you do *father* with any man, there is no connecting with them.

There's no likeness . . . they're not like you if they're taking care of you.

Alice: Yeah.

Fucking Master: How could they be like you? You see, the initial reason we grant our parents the ability to take care of us is because we know they look like us, we come from them, and, so, we accept that degree of likeness. But when you're dealing with someone who's your mate and not your relative or from your group, and you have them, or require

Are You Likeable?

them to take care of you rather than care for you, it becomes an unnatural position; an unnatural role. When we turn our mates into our parent or relative, people who have taken care of you, there's zero *likeness* and after a while you'll grow to despise one another.

Alice: Yeah, I completely understand that.

Fucking Master: We have to make an effort to connect *in likeness* to find the likeness that's inherent between us all. Once you've connected there, THEN we can finally start talking about something that matters . . . love.

You keep speaking of feeling sexy and I keep talking about being sexy.

Fucking Master

What is Sexy?

Fucking Master: What would the purpose of your life be if there were no men in this world? If there were no men in this world, what would you change?

Saundra: I wouldn't care as much about what I look like.

Fucking Master: I've watched a group of women together with no men around, where, after a while, they were not as concerned with how they looked. Think of a dormitory, a bunch of girls, no guys around, they eventually wind up living in their sweats. This would happen to you under the same circumstances. What does that say to you, then?

Saundra: That says I care too much about my looks.

Fucking Master: Or maybe it says more about the reason you care. What would be the meaning of your life if no man wanted you?

Saundra: I think that would be a freer life.

Fucking Master: Maybe. It would change though, right?

This alone shows the importance of men wanting you? It's good to be aware that you **need** men to want you. It then follows that if you need men to want you, in order to feel sexy, then you've passed the responsibility onto them. The burden is on the other. But what if it didn't matter to you what men thought of your looks?

Saundra: Then I'd feel freer.

Fucking Master: And does it have to matter in order for you *to be* sexy?

What is Sexy?

Saundra: If it didn't matter then I'd be responsible for feeling sexy, right?

Fucking Master: Yes. We can be sexy without it mattering. But it matters to you whether they want you or not. What does it mean to **be** sexy? You keep speaking of feeling sexy and I keep talking about being sexy. You need to understand that you can become sexy, you can express sexiness, you can enhance it, and you can repress it. It's energy, a force, a power. It's its own individual energy that we can tap into or not. It's the origin of where we come from. It's all creative energy. So, what makes you sexy or what makes you not sexy.

Saundra: If I can't even look a man in the eye for any length of time, that's not sexy, I don't think.

Fucking Master: No, unless you're playing coy. So, what makes you sexy?

Saundra: Being centered and comfortable.

Fuckin' Master: There are some *very* centered people who have no sexual energy coming out.

Saundra: Wanting sex.

Fucking Master: Wanting sex could add to it. But when you don't want sex can you still be sexy?

Saundra: I would think not.

Fucking Master: Then how do you explain a man being attracted to you, finding you sexy even when you don't want sex? Do you think that when Kate Upton doesn't want sex, men find her any less attractive, any less sexy? Or

What is Sexy?

Marilyn Monroe, in her time? Obviously not. On the other hand, there are women who want sex and appear as creepy as some men do. So, we need to question if wanting sex has anything to do with sexiness. Does it, in fact, create sexiness? Whether one desires sex or not, doesn't necessarily mean they're any sexier. So, let's look at other factors; what else makes you sexy?

Saundra: Well I can dress in a sexy way.

Fucking Master: So, we're talking about the physical body as an expression of sexiness. How you dress it and how you use it. What else makes you sexy?

Saundra: Confidence.

Fucking Master: Where does confidence come from? Because confidence is not something you just have, confidence is built. For instance, people get confidence from suddenly getting a bonus at work.

Saundra: If I think someone is attracted to me I feel more-sexy.

Fucking Master: That brings us back to "if there were no men wanting you," you wouldn't feel sexy. Remember, you're waiting for them to have you feel sexy. You're depending on them. Hence, this is why you don't feel free.

But what if you're wrong? What if being wanted is not where sexiness comes from?

What else makes you sexy?

Saundra: Youth and beauty usually does help.

What is Sexy?

Fucking Master: I believe Betty White is sexy. She's 90 years old and she's sexy. She can talk about sex. She calls her vagina a dusty muffin, and it's hysterical. Why is this 90-year-old woman able to talk about sex and not creep or gross me out while a 60-year-old woman can? What's the difference? We're talking about a 30 year difference here. So, why is Betty White able to do it; because it's not her physical body. Actually, I've even been creeped out by 30 year olds.

Saundra: Intent? Betty means to be funny.

Fucking Master: I get it. There are some people who mean to be funny and it's gross. What makes her sexy? She's sexy; men think she's sexy. She's hot. She's funny and hot. Would I want to have sex with her? No, but there's a lot of women I find sexy that I don't want to have sex with either. Did you know that? That it's possible to find someone sexy but not want to have sex with them? I don't want to have sex with her but it doesn't deny the fact that there's something sexual about this woman, something vibrant.

Saundra: I see the vibrancy.

Fucking Master: Yeah, and the vibrancy is not about mother. I don't go to Betty White for her to mother me. I go to her to hang out with her. I don't want her to play my mother, if I get to meet her. I want to listen to her jokes I want to hang out with her. Joan Rivers was another one; she was relevant into her 80's. I wanted to hear her. Hear her jokes; she was sexy in her own way. She was allowed. We allowed her, we allow Betty, we allow.

Now, let's take it out of the realm of comedy and look at, let's say…Oprah Winfrey. She's not funny, but she's sexy.

What is Sexy?

Oprah Winfrey's sexiness will come and go though, to an extent, all according to where she's at within herself. You see it can come and go with her weight changes but, again, only to an extent. She's too alive to extinguish it. She **is** in charge. You see you don't realize you're in charge of your sexiness. You really think its dependent upon a man. That's where your beliefs are off. You've depended only on whether they find you sexy or not to feel confident. You've got it a little ass backwards or back assward, as an old teacher of mine used to say.

Saundra: Its giving men power over me.

Fucking Master: You've relied upon two things: 1) being the nurturing mother and 2) over caring about what men have to say or think of you. This is an elementary black and white approach. There's so much more to discover and uncover about you. You try and rely on the mother part. If you dropped nurturing, and there were no men who wanted you, what would the purpose of your life be? I'm sorry to tell you, you'd have no purpose.

Saundra: Is that why I can't figure out what my purpose in life is?

Fucking Master: Yes, because you have these two blocks in the way.

Eliminate them and you'd feel lost . . . at first. But after a while, you'd see that you have a whole empty canvas to find purpose; to create purpose for your life.

Saundra: I've always thought there was a purpose but it was preordained.

What is Sexy?

Fucking Master: The problem with that belief is, then, your life has no free will. So you wait to be told what your life is all about and what your purpose is. So, your husband told you for a while and your kids told you for a while and now he's gone and they're just about gone. Now what? Who's going to tell you now what your purpose is? You made up that other people have to tell you what your purpose is. If you want to help people you can chose that as your purpose. Then you purposely help people. This is why nothing's changing fast enough. This is why we'll still be talking about this when you're 86 years old because you're waiting and it's not going to happen, because it's already happened. You've already lived out other people's purposes for you. You asked for freedom and so you got it. But you're not choosing anything because you think that one day it will come and hit you again. It will not, because you asked for freedom. You can choose purpose. What would you tell a daughter or a son who sat around the house and said "Mom I'm just waiting for my purpose to show up?" What would you think and say to them? That's what you're doing; you're just sitting on your ass like a lazy teenager. So you're not living, you're in wishful thinking. What does that mean, wishful thinking? Most of us have a lot of choice in purpose. Some don't have much choice; Michael Jackson, for example. His primary purpose was running through him well before he could even think for himself. That doesn't mean that he still couldn't have chosen a different purpose. Most of us are much freer than him, freer than a Mozart. They weren't' as free. For Mozart, this preordained purpose drove him a little nutty. He was practically a teenager his whole life; a mess. He never had a chance to choose his own purpose.

What is Sexy?

Most of us have the freedom to choose our own purpose. You asked for freedom and the predestined or other chosen purposes were removed; the one's others wanted for you. This wasn't from a divine choice. Your husband and the kids weren't a choice; they were someone else's choice or purpose for you.

Saundra: I chose them.

Fucking Master: For what purpose?

Saundra: For myself. I wanted to have children; I wanted to have a family.

Fucking Master: Well, let's start with marriage. Why did you choose marriage?

Saundra: For safety.

Fucking Master: There you go, it wasn't for you, and it wasn't freedom. So everything that follows from that, how can it be free? It's still clouded from what everybody else says and does. I wonder if no one else married would you want to get married? If you grew up in a world where nobody married, would you have wanted to get married?

Saundra: No, probably not.

Fucking Master: My old professor used to say we think we have choice, but even in Baskin-Robbins, where there are thirty one flavors, you still have no choice. It's been pre-decided the thirty one flavors. Even though it seems we have so much choice, know that even those thirty one are pre-decided.

What is Sexy?

Saundra: Are you saying if I have more than one to decide on I have a choice, but my choices are in a box?

Fucking Master: Some of us *choose* a mate; some of us *decide* on a mate. Can you wrap your head around that? What's the difference?

Saundra: Deciding, you're weighing the pros and cons and when you choose a mate you just choose.

Fucking Master: Good. So, in deciding, there is knowing; and knowing implies a previous understanding. How do I previously understand something I choose? I haven't had the experience of it yet. So there's no knowing in choosing.

Saundra: So if you go in and you've got thirty one flavors…

Fucking Master: Then the decision has already been made for you.

Saundra: But you can just choose one because you're choosing it, can't you?

Fucking Master: You can choose to stumble into that store. You can choose to not have any of the flavors, but as soon as there's a reason it's a decision. You want to question if a girl's mother says to her "I don't want you with that boy." What's going to likely happen?

Saundra: She's going to be with that boy.

Fucking Master: Is she choosing him?

Saundra: No.

What is Sexy?

Fucking Master: She's deciding against her mother's wishes. It's not a free choice. If her mother said nothing, she might be able to choose. We think we choose even the mates that we've chosen. In your case, Safety chose for you so you decided. Now, if you clear out all the need for safety you might have chosen that man . . . maybe. But we'll never know. This is not to say you wouldn't have chosen that man, but because safety was the issue, we know you didn't choose. We know you decided.

People have often asked me if we are predestined or do we have free will. My answer to them is always the same: yes. If you're asleep to your life, then everything is pre-determined; but if you're awake, self-reflective, then you have free will. Freedom implies choice; it operates unencumbered by previous conditionings. It trusts its lucidity in the moment. Its not that the past disappears; it's just that it doesn't do the choosing for you. You do. So when you think about what makes you sexy you think about all you've already known about sexy; all you've been taught.

So far, we know that men have made you feel more confident and sexy as has your dress and body movement, right?

Saundra: Yes.

Fucking Master: Well that's pretty limited, wouldn't you say? I think most teenage girls have figured that out, wouldn't you say? I must ask then, how much have you grown in the last three decades?

Saundra: Not much, apparently.

What is Sexy?

Fucking Master: Yes, but you're free now so you can grow. Explore now: what is sexy? I threw out Betty White to you. I'm saying she's sexy. Now what makes her sexy? Because it's not your definition, yet she's sexy. How is that possible? She doesn't have the body or the walk and she doesn't have men wanting her. How is it, then, that she's sexy? Think of a man who doesn't have the body any more, or the walk, that you consider sexy.

Saundra: I have a friend who's 65 now and he's still attractive.

Fucking Master: What is it that has him being sexy, then? Think of a famous person, for instance, like Helen Mirren. Most agree that she's still got IT. It's not her body for most men, yet she's sexy.

Saundra: I think Tom Selleck is sexy.

Fucking Master: Good; what makes him sexy, then?

Saundra: I don't know, I think it's his presence.

Fucking Master: That's it?

Saundra: Yes, I guess. What else could it be? He is older. He doesn't have the same looks anymore. Not everyone would be attracted to him.

Fucking Master: I agree, but again, that doesn't mean they wouldn't see him as a sexy older man. What else?

Saundra: I don't know; I can't see anything else.

Fucking Master: That's because you haven't looked any further. That would be like feeling warm on a cloudy day and saying it's because of some presence in the sky. No, if you looked past the clouds you'd see a sun and you would actually see that it's measurable. You'd see that it has rays, it's a ball of fire and it is made up of hydrogen and other chemicals. You could even figure out its specific origin. Therefore, if you can know the origin of the sun you can know the origin of sexy. You have a very narrow perspective on what's sexy.

That doesn't mean you can't be sexy in spite of not knowing. The problem is, as far as your purpose goes, if this is your perspective of sexy then you're not in control of your purpose. Instead, you're going to work very hard on making sure you walk right and dress right; this makes for an extremely hard life.

Saundra: I've been working on going out of the house more often without wearing make-up because I've realized it's too important to me. I've relied on it to the point where I developed great skill in creating perfect masks for different occasions.

Fucking Master: When you focus primarily on the outer mask, you can't develop the other areas that can have you increase sexy and there are a lot of other areas, internal areas. Apparently, Betty White worked on those areas. Where does this sexual energy actually come from? People have actually found the origin of it. It's not news. Your way of looking at it is what has most women miserable. How we look and walk and dress and what men think of us.

Saundra: That's what has most women do plastic surgery; chasing youth, obsessing over wrinkles, spending a fortune

What is Sexy?

on outfits and losing their self worth and dignity to what men want. Leaving them feeling like second-class citizens.

Fucking Master: You say you wanted freedom so **you** have a chance to get out of this craziness, but don't kid yourself. It's crazy. All the make-up in the world is not going to cover up crazy. Can you see how women start to look a little clownish and crazy when they try to use make-up to start covering it up because they haven't been able to figure anything else out? It's sad. The good news is you've chosen freedom; the good news is you can choose different purposes. The bad news is you don't have purpose without a man, or kids because those have been your purposes. Remember, being a nurturing mother is not sexy unless you find a man who just wants a mother and not a wife or girlfriend. They don't want a sex partner. Their wires are mixed, crossed, and they only want to fuck mommy. That's the only kind of man you'll attract if you approach as a nurturer first. The percentage of men who are this, is not large. So, you've really narrowed down your possibilities.

What you really want to ask yourself is "Where does my present day purpose originate from." Is it from your childhood or ordained from something deeper? Up to now you've lived the pre-destined life. There's no such thing as free will for you. Then, its just decisions on what's already been chosen. That's why you don't feel bad when you're given thirty one choices rather than two. It's still from what has been given to you that you decide from; you haven't given yourself anything. They have chosen it for you. Baskin-Robbins has chosen it for you. Coke and Pepsi have chosen it for you. Where's the new and creative?

What is Sexy?

Now, life is always changing, growing and expanding even if we're resisting it. It is clear that the universe is expanding, but you want to know, so are we. We've lived for centuries accepting that there are only two genders while, underneath the surface, there has existed intersex individuals all along.

Saundra: More than one gender? What do you mean by that?

Fucking Master: We are now expanding our perception and sexual identities that include other considerations and variations. We are beginning to consider that we are multi-gendered as a people.

There are people with both genders. It has been reported there are as many people born with both genders, as there are red heads in the world. Then there are transsexuals, people who decide to change gender; you can be both genders. There are individuals who have penises and breasts; those who have vaginas and a male body. They are a different gender. They are not male or female. Some researchers are saying that, five years from now, the Y chromosome won't exist any more so there won't even be men. It's starting to genetically get weaker. So, we're becoming multi-gendered. We don't know what it's going to look like because of evolution and what we choose. What we choose evolves. If we choose to spend most of our time in water, our bodies would eventually start changing. So, we don't have two genders any more, it's increased. Meanwhile, you have groups like the Christian's fighting tooth and nail to try to return to the two gender system. This is a losing battle.

What is Sexy?

Once in a while, we get these individuals who have really developed themselves. It's not just presence. They have chosen to "grow older" rather than "get older." They have looked inside and have chosen to include ***emotional bodybuilding*** into their daily regime. They encounter life, which allows their brains to grow, rather than live by what they've known, which causes the brain to become inactive. They question their belief's, preferring the truth over some be(lie)f. They look to be pulled until they find a flow. They've developed something that is so vibrant that sexy can't help but ooze out of every pore of their bodies. Yes, we can define exactly what sexy is; just like we can define its physical attributes.

Betty White is sexy, because she is *full of life*.

Beauty doesn't have to re-wow; it never stops being what it is.

Fucking Master

The Beauty

Fucking Master: I walked into the bank the other day and standing there, at the concierge desk, were these three attractive young women. Wow . . . this is already starting out like a cheesy joke; anyway, everything was okay until I took special notice of the middle one. She was beautiful! She was this exotic brunette beauty, gorgeous, tall and stylish.

I walked up to them to ask a question . . .

Trinity: I bet! (Smiling)

Fucking Master: No, (Laughter) . . . I actually needed to ask a question. I walked up to them, we exchanged pleasantries; I got the answer to my question and walked away.

Trinity: That's it?

Fucking Master: Yeah . . . that's it. What were you expecting?

Trinity: Well, you said she was beautiful, didn't you flirt or anything?

Fucking Master: No. I'm married, dear.

(Laughter)

No, I enjoyed the energy exchange . . . with all three of them, and then I moved on.

Danette: All three of them? I'm sure you paid a little more attention to the beautiful one; didn't you?

The Beauty

Fucking Master: No, why should I have? When I was young, dumb, and full of cum, I might have . . . but not these days.

Trinity: Losing that libido, eh?

Fucking Master: (Smiling) No. I just don't lose my shit anymore. I don't get thrown off like I used to with physical beauty. The reason being, I understand that beauty is rented. Understand? Physical beauty is a rental! The human being, who is objectively beautiful, doesn't possess it in actuality because all beauty is consciousness.

When I see a beautiful flower, hear a beautiful song, or see a beautiful and magnificent horizon I go, "Wow!" Beauty elicits that kind of reaction in me . . . in all of us. It brings up that *wow* moment, the moment where we get to witness consciousness. We are obsessed with the wow of human beauty. In my past, I would have believed that she possessed the beauty; that she was the source of it.

The other day, Danette, when you were talking about the *Khaleesi* character from "Game of Thrones," and we didn't agree that she was beautiful, you took offense. What's important to get here is that you didn't take offense on behalf of consciousness. What or who did you take offense on behalf of?

Danette: My own.

Fucking Master: And, what was that . . .

Danette: That it felt insulting to me to say she didn't possess this beauty.

The Beauty

Fucking Master: Whether you took offense on her behalf or your own, your offense was based on the belief that beauty belongs to the individual and is possessed by that individual.

We only rent beauty; we're allowed to rent it. It's not exactly a conscious choice, though. But somewhere on a soul level we chose to come into this world with *the possibility* of beauty; physical beauty.

Danette: The *possibility*?

Fucking Master: Yes, we can *destroy* it at anytime. This beauty we rented can be scarred and damaged, abused, or worse, by ourselves or others. We can cause it to be returned to its source.

Come on, the truth of the matter is that it's only going to last twenty or thirty or so years tops! And during that period it goes through a process to rise to a certain height and then it inevitably falls. That, in and of itself, proves that we don't own the beauty. Physically, beauty has a short, short lifespan; it's not for your entire life. It's only for a small period of your life.

A good example of this is Angelina Jolie. She was, undeniably, considered to be one of the most beautiful women in the world. But, today that opinion is beginning to change. She has, as of late, lost quite a bit of weight and has recently undergone a double mastectomy. Therefore, if you strip her naked, she's not going to look aesthetically pleasing to many, because of these reasons. She won't be the classic definition of beauty.

The Beauty

Beauty is short lived; we don't own beauty. SO when you took offense, somewhere you were in the belief that we own it and that I am offending both parties; you and the object of beauty.

Now, I can't offend the possessor of beauty because they are not the owner of it. In addition, I can't offend him or her who takes offense of my opinion of beauty because they misunderstand where beauty comes from. Their misbelief is what causes their offense; they don't understand that beauty is the territory of consciousness.

When I looked over at that young woman in the bank and thought "Wow," I was saying wow to consciousness; like "Great job!" That was me witnessing beauty. That's me, understanding that neither she nor I could own and permanently possess it. But, if I believed the opposite, then, as a man, I'd try and take it from her; as a man, I would try and take her beauty, sexually. This belief is what used to cause me to *lose my shit* in the past.

When I believe the opposite, I'm going to use her as a sex object. I'm going to sell her off to others or use her to build my business by utilizing her beauty. I'll have her sing, dance, or host my . . . let's say . . . restaurant business, right? I'm going to try and possess her, until her beauty is diminished or gone; then I'll dump her and look for the next *beauty*.

Or, I might be really greedy and want her to myself. I'll parade her around and show her off. I'll **take** her sexually. But, after a while, I discover that I'm having trouble possessing it, I need to have her again and again. "I need to own her. Yeah, that's it; I need to own her, so I'll marry her. I marry her because she's beautiful and I want to possess it."

Now, I own her and I don't want her to lose the beauty before I get to steal it, so I begin to put pressure on her to upkeep this beauty. I begin to see her as the keeper of the beauty; she's no longer the beauty and I put up with her. This continues until I stop seeing her completely; not that I saw her much in the first place, and I start treating her differently. I start getting used to her beauty. I'm in a fog and can no longer see the true beauty that is sourced from consciousness.

She can now be taken from me because others will be more aware of her beauty than I. I have fallen asleep to it, so I'm no longer witnessing. There's no WOW anymore, and the fact that she can't re-wow me, that she has to keep changing and doing things to wow me, proves that she doesn't own it because she can't will beauty.

Trinity: What it proves is you were an asshole!

(Laughter)

Fucking Master: Absolutely. As my wise old professor once said "An Asshole is someone who buys his own shit, while you don't." So, yeah, I've been an Asshole!

(Laughter)

Beauty doesn't have to re-wow; it never stops being what it is. The fact that a physically beautiful woman--we're not just talking women here, the same applies to men--the fact

The Beauty

that a physically beautiful woman tries to re-wow is silly; because . . . once again, the painful truth is she never owned it.

Now, what you need to understand is that the pain goes both ways. It's not just *the beauty* who suffers, but also her beholder. In my scenario, if I continue to buy the lie, I continue scrambling and trying to possess one beauty after the other while never finding satisfaction. I keep chasing until I've drained myself to death. Chasing beauty never ends well! Silly stuff, if you think about it . . . this beauty game; it's a really silly game that we play.

I've learned the truth about beauty, so I'm not thrown by a beautiful woman. Beauty is sourced, and the source is consciousness. Since I'm aware of this I can look further and see the woman behind the beauty. A beautiful woman doesn't get a pass from me because of her beauty; she has to show up with more than her surface. I'm not going to determine my connection to her based just on that, I have to see what else is there.

Beauty is something we're gifted with, like a beautiful voice. It's something the renter gets to have as a gift and is required to share, for the while that she has it, with the rest of us.

Danette: From the sounds of it, beauty doesn't seem to be such a great gift after all!?

Fucking Master: Oh, but it is . . .

Beauty and its fixating effect, its luring pull, remind us of our mortality and immortality, simultaneously. It provides hope to the hopeless and despaired. Above all, it has us recall the transcendent.

As for the renter, beauty provides her with numerous gifts, outside of the obvious. Like a magician who draws your attention away with his moving hand, while creating the magic with the other, beauty blinds you, thus allowing its tenant to develop from within. Because of the constant onslaught of attention, the renter is given the opportunity to develop muscles of discernment and insight. She's also able to distinguish the authentic from the inauthentic. Those who come to fawn over her, come unguarded. While they are busy projecting on her, she gets gifted with the opportunity to look deeply into their souls revealing to her the truths about the nature of Ego. Of course, everything I just said is impossible if she's unaware that she's more than her body.

If the *Beautiful* do no inner work, if they choose to be lazy and rely on their temporary beauty, no matter how much plastic and putty they put upon their bodies, they will lose it. Unless they're invigorated by an inner life, it will disappear leaving not a trace of its previous existence behind. Until science finds a way to regenerate us this will be the course we'll have to follow. Even if science does give us a helping hand, what's going to stop the ugly or apathetic internal will from revealing itself? So, if she doesn't take advantage and start building her beauty on the inside, it will fade and you will see what was previously hidden by that once beautiful shell . . . not only will it not be beautiful, it won't even be pretty.

The Beauty

The gift of beauty, if misused, will cost the renter tremendously. But, if she develops herself from the inside, while everyone else is distracted by the outside, then she will grow more beautiful than ever. Angelina Jolie seems to be doing just that.

Her commitment to her children, her *physical sacrifice* that allowed her to continue living so that her children could feel safe, her commitment to the well being of others, and her constant exploration of herself and her creativity . . . is creating a woman who is moving beyond her own self consumption. She is growing more beautiful and she is forcing us to see her as more than just a combination of parts. If she continues, she will become a *full beauty*; it will no longer be a rental.

You took offense for something that neither you nor the actress on the show own. You took offense to something that is temporary and a gift. Now if you're taking offense on behalf of consciousness, you don't have to! You don't have to defend *It*. But you might want to get outraged instead.

You could try to wake people up about beauty, but that's not where you were coming from. There was hurt in it, right?

Danette: Yes.

Fucking Master: Instead, you could have said "Hey let me enlighten you, Fucking Master; there's another way of looking at this. She's a different kind of beauty, a beauty that combines character from within with glowing exquisiteness from without. She may not fit into that classic definition of beauty that science says must be symmetrical, and measures it through a symmetrical box. No, she may not be a physically symmetrical beauty but she is a *harmonious beauty*." If you would have come forth with that argument, it would have turned out to be quite a different conversation . . . but that wasn't your argument! You were arguing as if you were the sole authority of what is beautiful or on behalf of an image of beauty you'd like to emulate.

Trinity: If you had come forth with that, at your age, I would have said you needed to get out more!

(Laughter)

The key is to understand that we cannot possess beauty.

Danette: If we can't possess it, then what are we supposed to do with it?

Fucking Master: We can *behold* it.

Do you know the expression *beauty is in the eye of the beholder*?

Danette: Of, course!

Fucking Master: What does it mean?

Danette: That what's beautiful is dependent upon who's *looking* at it. What's beautiful for one is not necessarily beautiful for another.

Fucking Master: Good! So, according to this expression, the beholder, or *looker*, has the power to affect, change, and

The Beauty

self-determine what is beautiful. That's a disempowering position we're placing beauty in, isn't it? Beauty, then, has to depend upon on our whims and moods. It can only be seen with our *eyes* . . . and that is where the problem lies.

Okay, now let's reverse it. Tell me what it means to you reversed. *The Beholder is in the eye of Beauty.*

Danette: Well, first there's only a single "eye." Beauty has only one "eye" and that eye, it's watching *the Beholder*.

Trinity: Actually, I would think that if there is only one eye that it's likely a strong one and it doesn't merely look or watch the beholder, but *sees* the beholder.

Fucking Master: Excellent! This is the key, to be in the eye of Beauty.

Imagine what it must be like to look through Beauty's eye; to look at each other through the EYE of Beauty? Imagine what we would look like?

Trinity: It reminds me of the old Beatle's song "Lucy in the Sky with Diamonds." There's a part in it that speaks of "a girl with kaleidoscope eyes." That's what it must be like to look . . . sorry . . . to *see* through the EYE of Beauty.

Danette: It would mean that I would be seeing, not just one part of *the beholder*, but multiple parts of him.

Trinity: Yes, and it would be in Technicolor!

Danette: Wow, like looking at all the dimensions of a person, all at once!

The Beauty

Trinity: Beautiful . . .

Fucking Master: Well let me take my Superman cape off because . . . *I'm no longer needed here.*

(Laughter)

When we are present to beauty through beauty, we are gifted with a "WOW" moment. It's Wow because we are witnessing something transcendent through the transcendent. To see through the eye of Beauty is to know that we can never possess it, we can never manipulate it, and we can never create it; although we should, ceaselessly, try to re-create it. It's to understand that it's a gift and that to be able to just touch it would leave us with great love and appreciation of it.

Danette: Is art our attempt to recreate it.

Fucking Master: You can say that . . . (Smiling)

We are all our own beauty . . . we are all potential works of Art!

You can admire it, which is non-touching; I admire beauties now that I'm married, right? I admire them, I might want to touch them but I have to keep it within the parameters of my relational commitment. But I understand I can't possess them. How could I posses your property if you don't possess it in the first place. How could I take possession of your home that you rent? I can't, someone else owns it, and that's what we do around beauty.

The Beauty

The point of all of this is to understand that any kind of physical external beauty all belongs to consciousness. But any beauty that you build from within, you get to own. You get to be a co-owner, an effort worthy of a lifetime of work; building inner beauty.

Everything else is a waste of time. It would be like me renovating this apartment that I'm renting. I'll only be increasing the value for the owner; I'll get nothing out of it! Do plastic surgery . . . but know that ultimately you're going to get nothing out of it; ultimately *you can't take it with you.*

Trinity: I see that with women who get false breasts, they really don't get anything out of false breasts. They treat them so impersonally.

Fucking Master: That's because they get to see that they can't possess them. They think that if they were natural they could possess them, but even natural breasts, a woman can't possess.

Trinity: I love the comparison of women's beauty to sunsets because we are so objective about a beautiful sunset. There have been times, Danette, where you have said, "WOW!" in amazement of the sunset and you've tried to share it when I've been preoccupied and I'll say something like, "Oh yeah . . . it's ok." You never take offense to that because you know you're seeing something that I can't see at that moment. But then your enthusiasm draws my attention and I want to know what is it you see that's so beautiful. And you're like, "Can't you see this . . .

how the clouds are floating and the colors blend?" and you bring out the beauty for me so that I can experience it.

We don't take offense, nor do we try to possess a sunset, yet when we speak about human beings, we take offense and we try to possess it. We place value judgments on what's right or wrong about beauty. I'll never see beauty the same way again out of this conversation.

Fucking Master: Beauty is from the realm of the Gods, it belongs to the Gods. It is shared with us. Whether it is shared through a sunset or in a mirror, it's helpful to be grateful either way. Like a sunset, our opportunity to witness it is temporary. It's silly to obsess about what you're seeing in the mirror, when life happens in a blink of an eye; you might miss most of it with this preoccupation. In addition, why are we, as a society, scrambling around trying to photograph everything if it isn't to possess beauty; trying to seize it from every right angle?

Danette, your generation has magnified vision. You are all so acutely aware of facial nuances and body positioning that you go around life like movie directors. You know what angle you need to be in to take a picture that shows you in the best possible light. You have creatively fine tuned it. But it's done, all in the name of possessing beauty. We cannot possess beauty, it belongs to the Gods. Even if I buy a Picasso and stick it on my wall I still won't possess it. Because I don't live forever! It belongs to the world! A beautiful being belongs to the world. When you try and cage a beautiful mind, or a beautiful heart, a beautiful face or body, you are committing a crime upon the world because it belongs to the world; it's meant to be shared.

The Beauty

You can see this playing out with envious and jealous people. Envy and jealously are considered vices, or deadly sins, that cause us to try and possess the beautiful; that which is meant to be shared and objectively experienced.

Danette: I think it's interesting that the popular term "she really *owns* her beauty" refers to a woman who spends a lot of her time on her outer self; her outer beauty.

Trinity: So maybe instead of owns, we can use the expression knows . . . or appreciates!

Fucking Master: Could it also mean that we experience them owning it when they start owning their inner beauty?

Danette: Well, that's probably how it manifested, from them working on their inner beauty, but most people don't see it that way usually . . .

Fucking Master: Maybe, like with Trinity and the sunsets, you can show me what you see? Well how do you see it?

Danette: I notice that I'm very sensitive to people's inner beauty so if there's someone who's externally beautiful and they haven't worked on their inner beauty, I can find them very unattractive. On the other hand, *Khaleesi* occurs to me as someone who has worked on her inner beauty. I feel certain energy from her. With those I don't feel that same energy with, I can't see their beauty; I only feel the inner ugliness.

Fucking Master: With a camera lens you can go close focus, distant, you can angle it, change the lighting, make it darker, and change the coloring with filters. We do similar things with our eyes. We can expand *the lens* of our vision to see only the basic physical beauty of a person or zoom in to *see* the possible deeper aesthetic beauty. When you look at the *Khaleesi* character, are you zooming in and actually including the actress herself, are you seeing Amelia Clarke; are you seeing **her** inner and outer selves? If you are then you're not wrong when you say she's beautiful.

Danette: The Beautiful is consciousness, you're saying . . .

Fucking Master: One can say that . . . (Smiling) True ownership can only occur from within.

Danette: So when someone's saying "she owns her beauty" could they actually be right?

Fucking Master: Only if they're speaking about the inner and outer.

Many people think that they own their *sexuality* because they get lots of attention. No . . . You don't own your sexuality by shaking your ass, your tits, or flexing your muscles alone. You must first surrender to an energy that is larger than you; you must give up control so it can express itself through you. In this case it's Sexual energy.

You can see this with dancers. There are many wonderful dancers out there, like beautiful people. But when a dancer has surrendered fully to *Music*, you know it. You're left with a feeling of peace and awe when you've witnessed a dancer's dance that was done in full surrender. You and the dancer become one and there is no doubt in that moment that he or she is expressing from a transcendent place; and

The Beauty

you're transcended with them. This is not what happens with most dancers.

For most dancers there is no surrendering because there's too much Ego. They may dance really well but they'll never transport you or themselves any further than the "Oooh, look at me" place. The same happens to the beauties of the world.

When a beauty has surrendered to the larger and has become *one with it, through appreciation,* then the acts of shaking their asses and tits and flexing their muscles become a thing to behold; it becomes a thing of beauty. This is not to say that a person has to be externally beautiful to do this, they just have to have had surrendered. Then and only then are you left with a WOW experience because a different energy is at play; an energy that confirms ownership. This is the energy I think you were talking about, Danette.

Danette: Yeah, that's it!

Trinity: I remember in the movie *Charlie Wilson's War*, there was this woman doing a belly dance that stunned me, because not only was she aesthetically beautiful but you could see she was bringing something forth from the inside. And these men in the scene, who were trying to conduct business, couldn't help but be entranced. They were pulled not just from her outer beauty but from what she was bringing from inside.

So, there she was shaking and moving just like any other belly dancer, or even stripper, but boy she was nothing like them, because there was a different inner beauty coming forth. So, don't be deceived by the external movement. We can mimic that, it doesn't mean you own it.

Fucking Master: When a woman possesses her sexuality and then *moves*, that's something extraordinary. She can no longer be a representative for others and she's not for rent. They cannot rent out her beauty by paying her a few bucks to go and be the face of a store, a strip bar, a brothel . . . or even a dance company.

A dance company, which is an artistic endeavor, often rents out men's and women's beauty to sell tickets. They don't have to be the best dancers. They'll take a lesser dancer, as dramatised in the play *A Chorus Line.*

When we're young, we hold the commonly held belief that we can possess beauty. This is what leads us to many degrading mistakes. We want to understand that if we knew better we'd do better. So it's important to know that we need to forgive ourselves. Forgive ourselves for renting, trying to sell, and being obsessed with beauty. The same goes with our sexuality; beauty and sex, of this persuasion, go hand in hand.

Why do you think many people stop having sex when their bodies change and/or the beauty disappears?

Danette: Because they feel undesirable?

Fucking Master: Kind of. They feel undesirable because they've related their looks with their sex; but one thing has nothing to do with the other. Unfortunately for them, they've collapsed the two. So, as soon as they start losing their looks they stop having sex! They never built an inner connection to their sexuality.

If you're only using beauty and sex to get attention, then your sex life will diminish with time. You will cease having a satisfying sex life. You will be too uptight about what you look like, and you'll start hiding or obsessing. And, if you're obsessing on beauty, it will use up so much energy and time there won't be any left for actual sex. You'll be working really hard to make your bodies look good but you won't have time to enjoy them!

So, to summarize this conversation, you want to know that beauty belongs to the Gods and it's only by communing with them that we get to own it. We all have the opportunity to experience beauty whether it's through our bodies, through others, or other things. Like the beauty of a rose which lasts a short period of time, or a mountain which lasts human lifetimes, or a sunset which lasts a few hours, it all belongs to the Gods and we get to be one with it. We can't possess those things, they don't belong to us but we can *become* them. At the least, they are to be appreciated, you're welcome to admire them, and they are to be embraced. Beauty allows us to connect, with enjoyment, to the consciousness that originates from within us all.

Danette: I'm just seeing how it would make such a difference when I'm choosing a partner because I wouldn't be so focused on their outer beauty. I'd be able to see more of what they actually possess, which is the inner beauty. That would be so much more attractive to me because I would understand that their outer beauty wasn't up to them, it was up to chance, or consciousness.

The Beauty

Fucking Master: For some people, chance is another name for consciousness. Excellent. So, then we can forgive ourselves for our past indiscretions. We just didn't understand we were coming from the wrong premise. If I thought the world was flat, I would be scared on a yacht. You can't blame me for that. I have the wrong conception of how the world functions.

Danette: But the depth of beauty that I can now find is infinite! It's been so limited because I was focused so much on the outer beauty.

Fucking Master: Now you can acknowledge variations and subtleties of emotional beauty, of mental beauty, of other physical beauties. Beauties like movement, vocal patterns, looks, and a smile. There are multiple layers of beauty, physical, mental, and emotional! When one starts connecting with the true spiritual energy that forms beautiful things, well . . . that can occupy us for several lifetimes, not just one. We waste so much of our lives on the physical, it's ridiculous, and sad.

Trinity: Why wait till you're 49, after your physical beauty has diminished or disappeared? Start looking at it now, at 24, and you'll become such a depth of beauty that people will be constantly saying WOW when they encounter you.

Fucking Master: A 49 year old that stands in front of the mirror to put make up on and puts it on with the intention of looking close to what she used to look like, is going to put make up on a very different way than someone who looks in the mirror and accepts the canvas they have to work with. She'll put on make-up completely different; she'll never put on too much as so many older women do.

Most women over 40, put on too much make-up, not just because of bad vision but because they are trying to recapture the old. Rather than work with what is, they've placed too much value on what was. But if they work with what is and look further inside to who they have become, and can continue to become, they're going to look BEAUTIFUL! Even those who have lived a shallow life; with this particular type of examination, of self work, they can still find a glimmer of beauty in themselves and others. They can begin to see through the *EYE* of beauty, through the *EYE* of I AM.

Why do we work so hard to create a safety that we can neither take with us nor really live life fully in?

Fucking Master

The Unholy Triangle

Fucking Master: How are you doing today?

Trinity: I'm feeling like crap.

Fucking Master: What about?

Trinity: I can't seem to get anything right or make anyone happy. I feel like I have no control over my life. When my kids are happy with me, my husband is not. When they're not complaining, then it's my boss who has it in for me. I can't seem to be able to keep anyone happy. One minute I'm the best; and in the next I'm the cause of someone's misery. I feel guilty even thinking this, but I can't wait till the kids are grown and I have less on my plate. Approval, disapproval, it feels as if I'm always on some sort of see-saw.

Fucking Master: Actually, it's a series of triangles that you ride on.

Trinity: Triangles?

Fucking Master: Yes.

Trinity: What do you mean?

Fucking Master: When we perceive life from a three-dimensional standpoint, we operate in forms of three and diminish everything else to two's. It is easier to look at two things at a time when we're a three because two is smaller than three. It's more manageable; especially when we're feeling vulnerable. When we feel unsafe, out of control, or disapproved of we need to believe we are larger than our lives to bring it back into balance. Otherwise, it becomes overwhelming. So we reduce the world to two, everything becomes dualistic.

Trinity: I think I'm following you; can you give me an example?

Fucking Master: Yes, rest assured that during this conversation you will alter between three states; Adult, Parent and Child. You will act accordingly, depending on which part is provoked. For instance, if I anger you, you may first go into child mode where you'll act like a brat to provoke my Parent self; this will allow you to get back at mommy or daddy. Or you'll switch to Parent mode, looking to possibly bring out my child part, where you can then attempt to take on a position of authority and overpower me. Finally, if all else fails, you may change over to the Adult state where you can take on more responsibility and accountability of your feelings. By the way, this whole process is best explained in Dr. Eric Burns book *"Games People Play"* if you're interested in looking further.

Now, let's look at your complaint.

You mentioned how you feel out of control and disapproved of.

Trinity: Yes

Fucking Master: How about unsafe, does this all make you feel unsafe at all?

Trinity: Definitely.

The Unholy Triangle

Fucking Master: Well, you want to know that these three feelings: feeling out of control, unloved/disapproved of or unsafe, or their flipsides--*think of them as coins*--wanting control, love/approval or safety, are the three blocks that keep us three-dimensional. They are the sources of all our three-dimensional pain, and when we are in this pain we tend to handle them predominantly from a Parent or Child mode. This, of course, makes it impossible to break out of it.

Trinity: So what do I do about it?

Fucking Master: First, we have to create some time and space to contemplate; a little down time or meditation can help with this. Then contemplate what life would be like without these feelings. Can you imagine life without them? What would it look like? That would be where a person should contemplate because if you can't contemplate it, if you can't see it, you can't change it. So what would life be like without those three?

Trinity: I don't know life without the three; wanting approval, safety and control. That's all I saw this morning. It's all I live in, and it just has me go directly to the future.

Fucking Master: It's a triangle that you live in; a triangle that has each of these three coins occupying its own individual corner.

Now imagine residing outside of this triangle. If you could, you'd see different options of behavior previously unavailable to you. Outside of it, you'd know that the "three coins" are just feelings. You'd know you are separate from them, outside of them. But living inside you

The Unholy Triangle

would eventually come to believe that you are them, you are these feelings. In addition, you can only see them dualistically as approval or disapproval, there is no other option.

I'd like you to imagine a parent who lives in the triangle and is afraid of disapproval and needs approval. Now picture them standing between these two extremes. Which side do you think they'd align themselves towards if their teenage daughter asked to do something that wasn't appropriate? Obviously, they'd align towards approval and play the "cool parent" role, which causes the opposite of what she's after. The daughter knows that her parent is weak to this pull, and because of this, she ends up disapproving of her anyway.

To *overcome* this pull we must keep still. This necessitates discipline and great presence of mind. It is a truly hellish battle, fighting the currents between the three lines of this triangle. To *transcend* this, we need to step out of it; there we can access our natural flexibility and fluidity. There we can *change channels* without getting stuck.

When we are inside the triangle, we are in time. Therefore, we could go *through* time into the past or the future. This is why you went into the future. This was how you gained temporary relief from this hellhole; a hell that would cease to exist if you weren't stuck in the triangle.

Outside the triangle there aren't any doors to walk through. This is where the adult and parent should reside. The child should reside and belongs **in** the triangle where they learn and grow safely; that's school for them. They can't walk in and out of it. The adult, on the other hand, needs to be able to teach and or parent; therefore, they must be flexible and that is only possible from the outside. Unfortunately, if an adult has not been properly parented, they wind up with an overwhelming need for family which causes them to take up all the space inside the triangle, leaving the next generation with an equally insufficient amount of space to grow.

Trinity: So they escape by going into the future or the past.

Fucking Master: Right. That's what they do and they do this while their children are watching them. Understand that children have never stepped foot outside the triangle. They are like fish in water; they don't comprehend the idea of past, present, and future. They don't experience the reality that an adult or parent knows. The child's reality is only in the now, which you do not want to confuse with the eternal now, but rather it's a limited now that is restricted by his parents consciousness, and he is left to conclude that something must be wrong with him since it is he that they are moving away from. These are the experiences that create lifelong abandonment issues.

When a parent is outside of time they're able to blanket their child's small world. The child never feels alone because of it. An effective parent is an adult who plays the role of parent. It's not who they are. Parent's who think that's who they are wind up in "The Parent Trap." In this trap there are only two places to escape to and that is the past or the future. Since your children have already left home and you are still in the Parent Trap, then your only escape is to let your family die; you **have to let your**

The Unholy Triangle

family die. The triangle is what you're locked in because of past parenting habits that no longer work in your new adult life. Presently, everyone's gone and just your habits are in place; you are parenting from your child parent state rather than as an Adult Parent.

Trinity: What I've been doing is trying to manage my own child from my parent.

Fucking Master: This keeps your child active and in the forefront. You've activated your own child so you can stay in what you're familiar with, triangular parenting. This provides the false sense of safety that keeps you spinning the three coins. There's no one else involved and I'm standing out here waiting outside of time . . . while time is disappearing for you.

Trinity: And you're saying that my pursuit of the "three coins" as you call it, is what's keeping me in the triangle.

Fucking Master: Yes, that and habits.

Trinity: So what now?

Fucking Master: Objective observation.

We need to acknowledge what part of ourselves is in operation. Whether it's our child or our parent, or whether we're in the pursuit or avoidance of love/approval, control and security. When we are in the triangle, run by these three coins, we can't be in time. There can't even be a realistic consideration of time. In addition, our experience of space is also distorted.

Space gets tighter if the space is within the triangle because it's not space *in time;* space in time can be expanded. Space is expanding right now in time. The universe is expanding in time. That's the truth. You're "truth" is that you want to limit space in time.

Trinity: Is that why I have to control space so I can control time?

Fucking Master: Yes, and vice versa, but, in the meanwhile you're never living in time only with it. Time allows space to be free, to be what it is. It's only when we're in time that we can encounter space; it's only in space that we can encounter time. In simply encountering them, choices are revealed. In time and space we choose freely and we enjoy this experience unencumbered by the coins because these coins can only exist within the triangle.

Imagine yourself living, one full day, without caring about security, love/approval, and control. It is hard for you to comprehend isn't it?

Trinity: Yes

Fucking Master: Yet, I'm sure you can recall a moment, or moments, when LIFE gifted you and moved you outside the triangle. I'm equally sure that you explained it away as prompted by love, *which you credited a man as the cause*, prompted by music, *which you credited the musician* rather than her muse, or a high prompted by drugs or alcohol, *which you credit them for*, or other transcendent phenomena, which you gave little thought to and just labeled as "weird" while never truly understanding its genesis. What happens after we return from these

The Unholy Triangle

experiences, is an eventual crash that leaves us with feelings ranging from apathy to despair, at which point we start chasing after or running from what we think initially caused or blocked the experience, thus, perpetuating the spinning of the coins. Because of these misplaced credits, because we credit things outside ourselves, we naturally feel a pull towards them in an attempt to re-establish this desired feeling that comes with being outside the triangle.

Once again, you don't know life without the three coins, so you give them greater power over you than they actually possess. You misunderstand that when you feel them, it doesn't mean you are them. They are just natural feelings that come and go. To understand this is to know and to then be able to say when they pass through, "Oh I'm temporarily insecure…" and keep going. "Oh look at me wanting control; okay let's keep going. Oh look at me wanting approval, let's keep going." We can take a different turn or approach because we'll know that on the *outside,* space is infinite; space is expanding. Presently, you don't get that space expands. You think space gets smaller as you age; no you get smaller because you're living life according to past experiences.

Trinity: I know, I have no vision for the future, I only have dreams and they change daily. And it's all in me trying to control time and space.

Fucking Master: That's because you need approval or disapproval, you need to feel safe or insecure . . . you need to feel out of control or in control. We make a mess, so we have something to fix. When you're outside of that triangle there's too much space to worry about making a mess; too

The Unholy Triangle

much to experience to worry about fixing anything or creating a drama--too much to do, too much fun, and too much to explore. Why reduce it? Why do we work so hard to create a safety that we can neither take with us nor really live life fully in? In your case, you try to recreate a small safe piece of heaven. Why are you rushing to the afterlife? You're missing out on this one.

This life is a limited experience, make the best of it. You will have infinity after that; you don't need to create it here. Such a waste of life you're living.

One night, when I was only a child, I closed my eyes and slowly counted to ten. When I reopened them it was daytime and I freaked out. I don't know what happened or how that happened or what I did and I never forgot it.

Trinity: It was night-time? And you said you were going to close your eyes and count to ten and when you opened your eyes it was daytime?

Fucking Master: Yes.

Trinity: So you expanded the whole hours of the evening. And you did this when you were in a meditation?

Fucking Master: No. I was a kid and I wanted to try things. So I tried that, and I willed it. I said I'm going to close my eyes and count to ten and when I wake up it's going to be daytime, and it bugged me the fuck out. And I didn't tell anybody.

Trinity: I immediately went to that you actually fell asleep in between then you're subconscious woke you up.

The Unholy Triangle

Fucking Master: That's what people say. But, I felt lucid the whole time. What likely happened was that I stepped outside the triangle, hence outside of time, and then I came back in. If you imagine all of time happening inside a transparent tube and you are standing outside of it, you'd see all of it is there . . . past, present and future . . . and you'd be present to it all at once. Now, the person living inside of it might take years to get to the end, to their death, but for you, it would be experienced in an instant; ten years, BOOM, an instant. A lifetime, boom again, only an instant to you. In the triangle, we experience and struggle with time and space, but just outside of it we can know it in an instant . . . or eternity.

So maybe when I counted to 10 I stepped out, while for you, if you were observing me, it took maybe eight hours. What if I stepped out of time? If I stepped out of the tube, walked around, and went in the other end it would just take me whatever time it took me to walk around, wouldn't it? So, when I went back in it was eight hours inside but outside it was only 10 seconds.

Please don't confuse this with when you disconnect, avoid, or wander off into your imaginings. When you do these things, you are not outside of time; rather, you're in a make believe matrix. It's like a purgatory; it's made up, it's inside the tube. Like a mental patient, you're lost in an illusion; insane. An illusion you've convinced yourself is reality. You cannot know yourself inside life. You must step out, even if it's just occasionally, to see yourself, to know yourself.

The Unholy Triangle

As soon as a person goes outside of the triangle they become lucid. This makes it easier to go back in lucid and to remain so, but to remain lucid does take additional effort. But a person who's never been outside of it is really just making shit up about what they know of life.

Trinity: Is that why people, who have had those outside of time experiences, come back with exceptional knowledge? Maybe like Nostradamus?

Fucking Master: Yes. Let's say Nostradamus was in fact a legitimate seer. Then, what likely happened was he stepped out of the triangle and saw that on or about September 11, 2001, two enormous structures would come crashing down causing tremendous pain. Upon his return he proceeded to describe, of course in metaphoric terms, how two mountains from a great city would fall. Because of the narrow mindedness of the time, it would have been too dangerous for him to have described it literally.

So you see, he didn't travel through time. No, he came outside of it. Nobody travels through time except for the people who are in it.

Trinity: Would you say, then, that stepping "outside" is the only way we can be self-observant?

Fucking Master: No, we can also reflect. Reflection is done "inside" the triangle.

But, firstly, let's address what is meant by self-observant. Self-observant, or the practice of self observation, is supposed to be the process of observing ourselves for greater self insight. The problem with this is that we are all

The Unholy Triangle

too quick to *judge* or try to *change,* whatever it is we have observed if it has made us uncomfortable or worse. Like old gunslingers, we carry around two guns called "Judgment" and "Change."

The *judgment gun* is the one we use when we don't like what we are observing about ourselves, while the *change gun* is the one we draw and shoot whenever we think we can change what we observed before it makes us feel badly. Therefore, it's objective observation that we want to practice rather than self-observation. Objective observation is the practice of observing ourselves *objectively*. That means to see oneself without judgment and without trying to change what we are observing, to just *simply* see without analysis. It is the practice of seeing what we're doing *in time*--now. For inside of time is where reflecting comes in.

Reflection is going inside and *seeing* the whole picture. It's a right brain activity. It's where one goes still and quiet in order to calm the mind. This calming of the mind, for reflective purposes, was explained in detail in the west by the old French thinker, Jean-Jacques Rousseau.

In brief, he explained how our minds are like a lake and that, when it is still, we can see a clear reflection of ourselves, others, and the world. This reflection provides the other half, the shadow side. With reflection we get to see the whole picture, effortlessly.

Trinity: I have had glimpses of awakening but the majority of my life is about approval, safety, and control. That's where I live. It's my reality. Hence I have to live in the future.

Fucking Master: Again, that's where you go to get a break. To get away from me and others, to get away from the pressures of disapproval, to get away from the pressures of creating security, to get away from feeling controlled. That's where you go. You see me, for instance, as a cause, you see me as the person that keeps, or sources, approval, safety, and control. I'm not interested but you group me with the rest of the *causers* because you live in a three dimensional world.

Trinity: When I'm in my adult it's easy for me to see the problem with living three dimensionally. But when I'm not, which is most of the time, I get easily caught up in its smallness. It's a tight existence with so much pressure.

Fucking Master: It's a pressure that you don't even realize you live under.

Trinity: Yeah, so why is it that I can see other's limitations better than my own?

Fucking Master: When you do, it's because you're not caught up in your own bullshit. You are in your adult where you can see you and the other clearly, and this is done objectively. This objectivity provides the adult greater depths of insight where they are then able to give better feedback. This ability can be used for, what you'd call, positive or negative purposes. This is what a con artist uses.

As my old professor explained, a con artist is someone who knows they're full of shit but you don't. They use their adult insight to see your weaknesses and play you accordingly. You, on the other hand, buy your own shit when you believe that the inside of the triangle is all there is.

The triangle is a very simple concept that you've complicated. You are trying to get a PhD in it. But, schools don't give PhD's on the triangle, unless you complicate it, because it's too simple.

Trinity: Is that what I've been doing?

Fuckin' Master: Yes, you're trying to master the triangle while still being in it. You think you can accomplish this by getting approval, getting safety, or getting control. No, you can't, but you can bullshit yourself that you can. You can buy your own bullshit which makes you, as the wise professor said, the definition of an ASSHOLE.

www.ingramcontent.com/pod-product-compliance
Lightning Source LLC
LaVergne TN
LVHW051503070426
835507LV00022B/2905